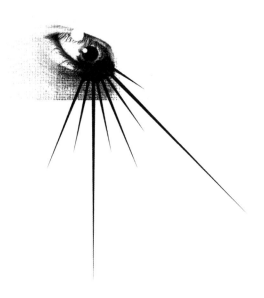

Alessandra Vaccari

WIG WAG . The Flags of Fashion

Marsilio   FONDAZIONE PITTI DISCOVERY

translation
Huw Evans

graphic design
Alessandro Gori.Laboratorium

cover
Photo by *The New York Times Magazine*, edited by Stéphane Sednaoui

Fondazione Pitti Discovery apologizes and is available if any photographic credits
have been unintentionally omitted

First edition: September 2005
ISBN 88-317-8802-7

Distributed in the UK and Europe
by Windsor Books
The Boundary
Wheatley Road
Garsington
Oxford OX44 9EJ
Tel. 01865361122 Fax 01865361133

CONTENTS

INTRODUCTION

Fashion feels at ease within the constraints imposed by a theme. It is capable of weaving all sorts of stories around it. It is able to develop the cues provided by a trend, tracking down the guiding motivations of a collection and bringing into focus the ideas on which to build an advertising campaign, a photographic service or a window display. In fashion themes are used to communicate certain moods, to guide research and the creative dynamics of design and to trigger processes of self-representation in labels and people. Themes form the hub of a rich stylistic phenomenology that reflects the continual transformation of the representations of fashion, confirming its central role. From this strategy dear to fashion I have borrowed the thematic narrative constraint utilized in this book, which unfolds in an oscillation between fashions and flags. When I speak of fashion I am referring to its twofold nature as a creative process – in the aesthetic and anthropological sense – and as the organization of this process into a system, where the production and diffusion of new clothing coexists with the creation of new cultural images and practices. It is what Elizabeth Wilson defined as a 'magical system' in her book *Adorned in Dreams* (1985) owing to fashion's ability to exercise its own extraordinary powers of illusion.

The theme of flags began to take on a new substance for me when I realized that it was something more than a potential way of tackling such critical questions as style and national identity, fashion and emblems of power, transnational cultural paradigms, ethnicity and representation of the self. The theme also offered me the possibility of embarking on a critical discourse, without losing sight of the visual spectacle and imaginative capacities of fashion design. I think that nowadays it is desirable for anyone setting out to interpret fashion not to stick to an attitude of critical detachment, but to leave room for the expression of his or her own ideas. In her *Fashion at the Edge* (2003), Caroline Evans suggested that in the study of fashion it was important to identify 'a language and a methodology [...] that did not eclipse fashion with theory'. The theoretical work carried out in recent decades has focused chiefly on the discourse of fashion, rather than on fashion in itself. The language and instruments developed in the sphere of fashion studies have not always attempted to tackle the tangible, decorative, superficial qualities of the forms and images of fashion. The tangible qualities it uses to express itself have often been dismissed as being of scant theoretical significance to the process of revising the traditional historical and artistic approach to fashion, an approach whose empirical and excessively descriptive nature has been criticized. These qualities have often been pushed into the background because they are considered too transient: a set of minute rules of expression in a grammar that is continually being rewritten. In other cases, however, they have been utilized in an illustrative (if not instrumental) way to confirm a certain theoretical framework, or rendered uniform through the category of textuality. By placing everything on the same level, the latter suspends judgement on questions of creativity, aesthetics and taste, which are vital for fashion itself. Although the logic of 'everything is text' tends to cut itself off from problems of beauty and taste, its application to the realm of fashion studies has had the merit of broadening the concept of fashion itself, by including within it not just the creative skills ambiguously reflected in the economic dividing line of high-priced goods, but also the 'lower' aspects that are pushed to the sidelines in traditional analyses of fashion from a historical and artistic perspective. At the same time, the logic of deconstruction has left a profound mark on the history of art itself over the last few decades, widening its field of interest to embrace anonymous forms of everyday creativity, reconfiguring the identity of the discipline or even breaking it down altogether, as in the case of studies of visual culture. This joint expansion of cultural interests in fashion, and the possibility of getting the positive aspects offered by fashion studies and the history of art to converge in a single approach, allows us to look simultaneously at the discourse of fashion, its creative processes and the forms in which such processes find expression, be they clothes, ornaments, images, labels or bodies.

Moving within this horizon, in the chapters that follow I shall investigate questions of identity and style that are implied by the relationship between fashion and flags, seeking to reflect at one and the same time on nationality, ethnicity and aesthetics. In doing so, I propose to keep turning to the world of fashion, in order to look at the infinite ways it makes use of flags from the viewpoint of design and visual culture. What interests me in particular is to reflect on the at once squint-eyed and all-embracing gaze of fashion. Its squint allows me to focus attention on a single theme, rendering the rest temporarily invisible. The breadth of its gaze will help me instead to reflect on the condition of fashion as at once spectator and shaper of the settings in which we live. The thematic strategy interests me, finally, for the light it throws on the creative possibilities offered by the juxtaposition of the old and the new and the combination of different references, tracked down inside and outside the boundaries of fashion. It is also this strategy that determines the historically and chronologically discontinuous approach I have decided to take. From a narrative viewpoint, in fact, the book is not organized in terms of a consistently evolutionary tendency, but follows the oscillating movements of fashion in its recurrent flirtations with the theme of flags. It is these movements that have inspired the title *Wig Wag*, signifying both to twist about and to send a signal by waving a flag or some other object.

DRESSING IN FLAGS

Flags are always available and easily identifiable inside and outside
the places they represent: concrete places and common places, utopias
and stereotypes. They loom over state ceremonies, the fronts of hotels,
the entrances of trade fairs and amusement parks. They flutter over
scenes of war, peace demonstrations and stadiums on Sundays, and are
even worn by people. Omnipresent in our world, flags fill the pages
of magazines and the screens of televisions and cinemas. They
produce a continuous flow of images, migrating without a pause from
reportages to dramas, from documentaries to fashion photographs.
This range of fragmented and often ambiguous visions has fostered
the development of theories about flags from a post-modern
perspective that blur the confines between aesthetics and politics,
putting style and contents on the same level. This is what the
historian of art and fashion Richard Martin has to say under the entry
'Flag Clothing' in the *St. James Encyclopedia of Popular Culture*:

In the United States, flag clothing is highly subjective; it can be either seditious or patriotic,

depending upon context. Radical Abbie Hoffman was arrested in the disestablishment year
1968 for wearing a flag shirt; beginning in 1990, designer Ralph Lauren had knitted or applied
the flag into sweaters and sportswear almost as a brand logo, and by 1995, so had designer
Tommy Hilfiger. [...] Critics continue to ponder whether flag clothing amounts to desecration
or exaltation, whether it's equivalent to flag burning or flag waving.[1]

The uses of flags are not always so unselfconsciously ambiguous as the
ones described by Martin in the United States. During the first
Intifada between 1987 and the early nineties, the vulnerable
Palestinian flag could not be flown freely over the territories occupied
by Israel, but was embroidered directly onto clothing along with
slogans in support of the nationalist cause. Given the serious nature
of such a case, the new orthodoxy of a progressive erosion of the
boundaries between the patriotic, ironic and critical use of flags
might irritate some by its propensity to place everything on the same
level. Yet it suggests the idea that flags are now complex and
fluctuating forms of cultural expression, an interpretation to which I
will constantly refer in the chapters that follow. Such an analysis, in
fact, seems the most appropriate when we set out – as in this case –
to consider the presence of flags in our wardrobe, where they appear
in the form of printed fabrics, embroideries, applications, crests and
badges scattered in profusion over garments and accessories.
The colours of one's own nation may be worn with pride or deference
to express a sense of patriotism, to meet professional obligations or to
demonstrate a political and sporting allegiance. Wearing the national
flag makes it possible to create an instant map of visual identity: this
is a practice that has as much to do with creative processes as the
dictates of fashion, although they do not exhaust its implications. An
example taken from the world of sport helps to show that the
question of dressing in flags extends beyond matters of fashion and
that the latter is not alone in exploiting its ambiguity of meaning
and fluctuating associations. In the early months of 2005, the Indian
government banned the use of the national tricolour on the helmets

Batsman Sachin Tendulkar during an India-Australia test
match, October 2004. Photo by Kamal Kishore
© Kamal Kishore/Reuters/Corbis/Contrasto

Italian football fans at Italy-Bulgaria match, 22 June 2004.
Photo by Martin, © Presse Sport/Grazia Neri

Dolce & Gabbana, spring/summer collection 2005

of the country's cricket team, on the eve of a series of important
international matches with Pakistan. After protests and diplomatic
negotiations conducted by the Board of Control for Cricket in India
(BCCI), the government eventually agreed to allow the use of a
simplified version of the flag, limited that is to the horizontal bands
of the saffron, white and green tricolour, but without the symbol of
the wheel (*Ashok Chakra*) that appears at its centre. To many the
sudden prohibition appeared unwarranted, especially in view of the
fact that cricket is the most popular sport in India and that the link
between sport and nation has always been very strong, as supporters
from all over the world demonstrate by painting their faces in the
colours of their respective national teams. Since 1947 – the year of
Indian independence from British rule – this sport of colonial origin
has progressively come to embody the nationalistic sentiments of the
country. This has been pointed out by Arjun Appadurai in his
analysis of cricket as a driving force in decolonization and an
important factor of modernization. According to this anthropologist
of Indian origin, cricket has been transformed into a great national
passion through the joint action of the public and private spheres:
coverage in the media is guaranteed by the state, while private
companies provide massive investments in the form of sponsorships.[2]
The current ban on using the flag on the uniforms of athletes is
officially justified by the government as an act of respect for the
symbol of the nation and the laws that regulate its use. This
interpretation takes on a different significance if it is seen in relation
– as the national daily *The Hindu* suggests – to the litigation
underway between the BCCI and government over the control of the
television rights for cricket matches.[3] Thus nationalistic extremism
shades into the contemporary dynamics of commoditization of the
sport and flag. Such dynamics are far more explicit in other countries.
While people in India seek explanations for the government's
decision, in Italy Dolce & Gabbana have set the tricolour badges of

the Italian national team on the hats, vests and slips of their menswear collection for spring-summer 2005. Thus the image of the Italian flag has been utilized to commemorate the nation's link with football and evidently with fashion, without incurring prohibitions or censure. Another striking confirmation of this is provided by the General Staff of the Italian Air Force, which has authorized the Cristiano di Thiene label of the company of the same name to produce and market a line of clothing with the official emblems of the national acrobatic team known as the Frecce tricolori and the air force itself. The perpetuation of forms of appropriation of national flags by fashion suggests that they are not the last shreds of now remote heraldic symbols, but continue to be disquieting emblems of power, objects of fetishistic veneration and alluring stereotypes of identity.

The Japanese military banner in the form of a rising sun with sixteen stylized rays on a white ground is a particularly popular graphic motif that is widely used by industry and fashion, partly due to its association with the post-punk tendencies of the early 1980s. In that period, Japanese military insignia became part of a Neo-Jap Style made up of kamikaze headbands, ideograms, back-combed hairstyles and elaborate geisha-style make-up. Examples of this are provided by Siouxsie Sioux, the singer of the Banshees, and by Donatella Rettore at the time of her record *Kamikaze rock'n'roll suicide* (1982). In 2001, however, the dress decorated with the rising sun worn by the Chinese actress and pop star Zhao Wei was taken by her fellow countrymen and women as an affront, reminding them of a troubled chapter in the history of China: the invasion and military occupation of its territory by the Japanese empire in the 1930s. Zhao Wei wore the dress with the rising sun for a photographic service devoted to the latest trends in international fashion compiled by the editor Zou Xue for the September 2001 issue of the Chinese magazine *Fashion* (*Shizhuang*). The service was set in a city symbolic of

Cover of Donatella Rettore's *Kamikaze rock'n' roll suicide*, 1982

Donatella Rettore, 1982

Zhao Wei. Photo Dah Len, in *Fashion* (*Shizhuang*),
September 2001

cosmopolitanism, New York, and the celebrity photographer Dah Len (commissioned to take the pictures) along with the brands of clothing that appear in the service, including Diesel, Helmut Lang, Levi's and Louis Vuitton, were of international standing. The dress with the Japanese military emblems was produced by Heatherette, 'a galaxy of fun and fashion' according to the slogan of this label founded in New York by Richie Rich and Traver Rains, young designers linked to the city's clubbing scene, MTV and personalities from the world of entertainment. After the service came out, the photograph of Zhao Wei was published by numerous Chinese newspapers and websites, which initiated a smear campaign against the actress-singer. Launched on 3 December, the campaign caused a great stir, as is demonstrated by the thousands of offensive messages sent to the website sina.com, the petitions from survivors of the Nanking Massacre in 1937, the lack of understanding on the part of the community of historians, the boycott of Zhao Wei's songs by the Suzhou Music Station and the investigations carried out by the China News and Publishing Authority. The controversy was brought to a conclusion on 10 December with a letter of apology from the actress, Zou Xue's promise to resign from his post at the magazine *Fashion* and after the explanations that both the photographer and Richie Rich of Heatherette felt it necessary to provide. The latter asked the Chinese public to take into consideration his perspective as a fashion designer and the fascination of Western youth with an idea of Asiatic culture that did not make much distinction between China and Japan. He also declared that he had never imagined an interpretation in an imperialist and anti-Chinese key, explaining that the motif of the flag on the dress was flanked by several Chinese words signifying the opposite, i.e. celebrating peace, joy and health.[4] Between the logic of fashion and anti-Japanese feelings, the Zhao Wei affair underlines the iconic power of flags and the global flow of images and messages they are capable of generating. Misunderstandings and conflicts bear

witness in addition to the collective emotional involvement produced
by the act of displaying a flag on one's body. This can be done with
clothing, as in the case examined, but also with tattoos and hair
sculpted and dyed in the colours of nations, political parties and
sports teams. Wearing a flag on your own skin is the most direct way
of displaying feelings of ethnic and cultural allegiance. In Europe, the
German flag is perhaps the most eloquent example of how the colours
of a nation have repercussions on the conscience of its citizens. After
the Second World War, the black, red and gold tricolour of the
Germans has reflected a sense of shame rather than patriotism. Only
today has this flag begun to present itself in a new guise, gradually
emerging as a European symbol of antimilitarism. Thus the fondness
for military shirts with a little German flag sewn onto the arm is
something more than a collective mania in the early years of the new
millennium. It is concrete proof that German army surplus can be
sold to stockists of military clothing and is also a way of expressing
support for the German refusal to endorse the war against Iraq
launched by the United States in 2002. It is in this context that we
should see the case of the German Eva Gronbach, who has based her
work as a fashion designer on a revision of her country's identity.
After her début collection *Déclaration d'amour à l'Allemagne*
('Declaration of Love to Germany') in 2001, she produced another
with the same title but in German, *Liebeserklärung an Deutschland*
(2002), followed by *Mutter Erde Vater Land* ('Mother Earth Father
Land', 2003) and *Meine neue deutsche Polizeiuniform* ('My New German
Police Uniform', 2004/05). The recurrent motifs of these last
collections are the black, red and gold tricolour and the symbol of the
eagle – which is also the logo of her line of clothing – utilized to
convey a new and peaceful image of Germany, as the historian of
fashion Ingrid Loschek explains.[5]
Wearing the national colours is, in the end, a metaphor for existence.
From the birth certificate onwards, life unfolds beneath a flag,

Kirsty Hume. Photo by Tim Walker, 1998,
from Colin McDowell, *Fashion Today*, Phaidon, London 2000

Eva Gronbach, *Meine neue deutsche Polizeiuniform*
('My New German Police Uniform'), autumn/winter
collection 2004/05. Photo by Boris Breuer

although this can vary in colour and design when we change countries, itineraries of travel, airlines and destinations. Even the new cultural paradigms based on transit have left intact the power of these emblems, which seem inevitable as indications of nationality on passports. Instead of vanishing, they are multiplying, along with the flows of migration and the shattering of the idea of the fatherland as a mythical territorial unit.

Flags are also the last garment ever worn, at least for some. They become the shrouds that wrap coffins in the solemn ritual of state funerals, where they represent the nation and its soil. Flags are the heart of the ceremony and an integral part of the pomp of this kind of event which, increasingly media-oriented, is staged for martyrs, war heroes, heads of state, kings, queens and princesses like Lady Diana. In the days following the car crash in which the princess of Wales was killed on 31 August 1997, the interest of the media and the public was caught by the organization of the funeral that would celebrate the last act of her existence. Apparently a secondary detail, the ceremonial of the flag in fact became the protagonist of the event, as the art historian Nicholas Mirzoeff has pointed out. He describes the funeral of Lady Diana as a clash between different images, protocols and symbologies: the Royal Standard on one hand and the Union Jack on the other. Like the divine, the monarchy never dies and – in compliance with protocol – the Royal Standard must always fly at full mast above the place where the royal family is in residence. Vice versa, the convention that the national flag should be flown at half mast as a sign of mourning was not permitted. So in the days following Diana's death, the flagstaff of Buckingham Palace remained sadly bare, while at Balmoral Castle in Scotland – where the queen had retired following the tragic event – the royal flag continued to fly at full mast. This was interpreted by the British tabloid press as a lack of respect for the princess and for the popular expression of grief, generating a tension that did not die down until the afternoon of

Alessandra Vaccari

Funeral of Lady Diana, 6 September 1997
© AFP/Grazia Neri

President Carlo Azeglio Ciampi at the ceremony to receive
the coffin of the officer Nicola Calipari, 5 March 2005.
Photo by Vincenzo Pinto, © AFP/Grazia Neri

4 September when:

it was announced that for the first time in its history, the Union Jack would fly at half mast at
Buckingham Palace during Diana's funeral. [...] The queen may even have thought that her
curtsey before Diana's coffin had been the final act of respect, but the biggest concession had
already been made with the flag at half mast.[6]

In view of the controversy over the flag above the royal residences,
the unanimous desire to see Diana's coffin draped in the royal
standard stands out even more clearly. On this, in fact, there was no
divergence at all between the popular point of view and that of the
monarchy, which showed no hesitation in honouring the memory of
the princess in a royal manner, even though her divorce from Prince
Charles and her consequent renunciation of the title of Her Royal
Highness should have prevented it. From the moment her dead body
was brought back from Paris (where the accident had taken place) to
the day of the funeral, Diana was wrapped in the heraldic
magnificence of an exceptional shroud. Transformed into an icon of
popular devotion, her image continued to appear all over the world
even after her death, confirming her destiny as the most
photographed and glamorous princess of the 20th century.

NOTES

[1] Richard Martin, 'Flag Clothing', in Tom Pendergast, Sara
Pendergast (eds.), *St. James Encyclopedia of Popular Culture*, vol.
II, St James Press, Detroit 2000, p. 111.
[2] Cf. Arjun Appadurai, *Modernity at Large. Cultural Dimensions of
Globalization*, University of Minnesota Press, Minneapolis-
London 1996. The passage has been translated from id.,
Modernità in polvere. Dimensioni culturali della globalizzazione,
Meltemi, Rome 2001, p. 139.
[3] 'Flag issue: BCCI to approach Govt.', in *The Hindu*,
23 February 2005,
www.hindu.com/2005/02/23/stories/2005022302641900.htm

[4] Richie Rich's declarations are given in the letter of apology
from Zou Xue, published under the title 'Unintentional Hurt.
[Fashion] Magazine Chief Organiser Zou Xue issues statement
of apology' in *Sina Entertainment*, 10 December 2001. The letter
is available in English at the address:
www.zhaoweinetfamily.com/news_e/news_e455.html

[5] Ingrid Loschek, *Mother Earth Father Land.
Not Uncontroversial - Eva Gronbach and Her Collections*,
Goethe Institute, July 2004,
www.goethe.de/kug/kue/des/thm/en138594.htm

[6] Nicholas Mirzoeff, *An Introduction to Visual Culture*, Routledge,
London-New York 1999. The passage has been translated
from id., *Introduzione alla cultura visuale*, Meltemi, Rome 2002,
p. 353.

DISTIⱭCTIVE DESIGⱭ

Flags visually mark the borders of a real or imaginary country. They associate brilliant colours with simple graphic schemes in a distinctive design capable of ensuring their absolute uniqueness. Ambiguities are not admitted, although certain colours or motifs recur from one flag to another. Each flag has its own history and a specific code of honour that governs permitted uses and the ones that are punishable by law. Unlike coins and banknotes, flags are univocal, in the sense that their front is usually the same as the back. But this rigid iconography does not limit their circulation. They can be reproduced without losing their authenticity and without committing the offence of forgery, as happens instead with the falsification of banknotes and trademarks. While it is relatively easy to appropriate the emblems of a nation, it is impossible for anyone to lay claim to their exclusive ownership. Since their existence is public, flags are visually democratic and function as an open source on which everyone can draw: fashion designers, musicians, athletes and fans with their faces painted in the colours of the national team.

Paul Smith, *Untitled (Fans)*, from the series *Sing
When You're Winning*, 2000, Lambda, 65 × 90 cm
Courtesy Robert Sandelson, London

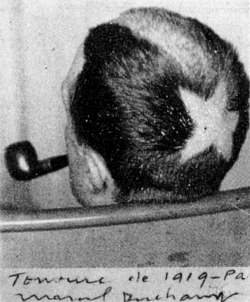

1261

Marcel Duchamp, *Tonsure*, 1919, photograph, 8.8 × 7.8 cm

Alessandra Vaccari

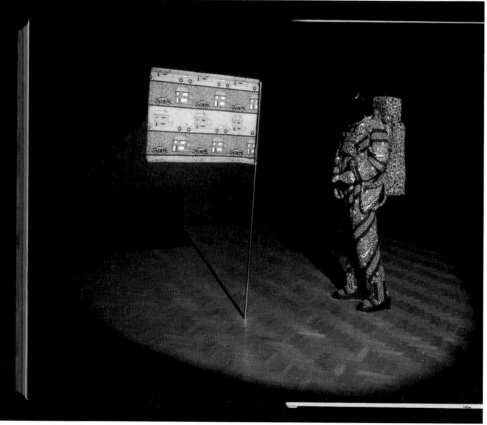

Yinka Shonibare, *Cloud 9*, 1999/2000, wax, printed cotton,
fibreglass, staff and flag. Astronaut 212 × 63 x 56 cm,
flag 183 cm
Courtesy Stephen Friedman Gallery, London; Neuberger
Barman collection, New York. Photo by Andy Kate

From this set of reasons stems much of the fascination exercised by flags, whose distinct graphic and geographic confines seem to encourage, rather than limit, the infinite forms of appropriation, reworking and travesty to which they are subjected. The focus of this chapter is on the ways in which the uniqueness and the visual immediacy of national flags enter into creative processes in the omnivorous imagery of contemporary culture. Both art and fashion continually make use of the images offered by flags, setting in motion processes based on appropriation, i.e. on the adoption of existing forms and the development of new forms of utilization of their public image. In cultures of appropriation, the formal qualities offered by flags can be acquired and adapted to new uses, playing on the shift in the context (from the national to the artistic) and the narrative (from the relative inertia of the patriotic message to the dynamism of its consumption, reiteration, boycotting, criticism and so on). Both art and fashion rely on feedback, amplifying the fluidity of meaning of flags and causing them to waver between nationalism and anarchy, utopia and dream visions, rather than assigning them fixed interpretations. This attitude has accompanied the entire creative history of the 20th century, commencing with the avant-garde movements of the early 1900s and the manifestos of the Futurists. Among the latter, *Il vestito antineutrale* ('Anti-Neutral Clothing'), signed by Giacomo Balla in 1914, is a form of appropriation of the Italian tricolour and its transformation into a living flag. In Futurist and Marinettian aesthetics, the green, white and red 'anti-neutral' suit was a symbol of the militaristic patriotism that heralded the entry of Italy into the First World War, but it was also an ironic strategy of style and colour to combat the grey mediocrity of menswear. In her collection for the summer of 1939, inspired by the idea of Paradise, Elsa Schiaparelli drew instead on the emblems of the Vatican State and the Catholic religion, embroidering the motif of St Peter's keys on a 'divine' evening dress.[7] The reasons for this can be sought as much in Schiaparelli's Roman origins as in the visionary propensities of this fashion designer.

Acts of appropriation of national flags have become common practice, especially over the course of the last fifty years, with the emergence of popular culture and its iconography saturated with stereotypes to be reactivated. Over this period, the process of permanent reinterpretation of already existing forms like flags has been extended to every area of the cultural industry: from visual art to cakewalk fashion, from the visual aspects of pop-rock to streetstyle and the daily practices of reinvention of the visible self. In an article published in 1967, the writer Angela Carter described the transfiguration of the Union Jack from a national symbol into a pop icon:

> When Pete Townshend of the Who wore his jacket cut out of the British flag for the first time, he transformed our national symbol into an abstraction, in a far more effective way than Jasper Johns did when he reproduced the American flag in a painting and hung it on the wall. The point is not whether Townshend was fully aware of the nature of his abstraction or not; he was driven by the pressures of the day.[8]

The jacket cut out of the British flag was in fact worn by John Entwistle, another member of the Who, as can be seen on the cover of the album *My Generation*, released in December 1965. But what matters is the transformation of the Union Jack, a process through which 'hitherto sacrosanct images are desecrated', continues Carter, but also rendered innocent by the 'purity of the style'.[9] Through the combined action of music, design and fashion, in the years of Swinging London the British flag became the coolest and most exportable emblem of youth culture and its stylistic values. A process that did not stop at the Who and the mods with the flags that they displayed all over the place, but extended to things that were not British at all: from Italian-designed scooters to the parkas of the American army. The Union Jack was confirmed as a guarantee of the

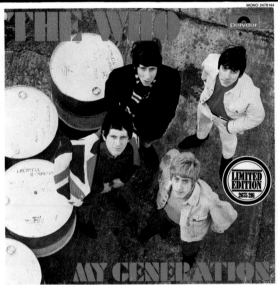

Cover of the Who's *My Generation*, english edition, 1965

The 'crazy wardrobe of twenty-year-olds' in 1966. From the
weekly italian magazine *Epoca*, in Giannino Molossi, *Liberi tutti:
Venti anni di moda spettacolo*, Mondadori, Milan 1987

Dennis Morris, *Untitled*, 1977, Virgin Record Shop, Notting
Hill Gate, London - first day of release of the *Never Mind the
Bollocks* album by the Sex Pistols
© Dennis Morris

Cover of the Clash's *The Clash*, 1977

Bratz *Pretty N'Punk* collection, 2005.
Distributed by Giochi Preziosi, GIG division

Fake London, spring/summer collection 2002

vitality of the British scene when it came to music, fashion, graphics and transgressive styles with the punks of the second half of the seventies. The image of the torn and perfunctorily reassembled flag, held together by safety pins and paper clips, was used by the graphic artist Jamie Reid for the poster for the Sex Pistols' first single *Anarchy in the UK* in 1976. From that moment on, the same flag appeared repeatedly in the promotional material devised by Reid for the Sex Pistols, and was even worn by Paul Cook – the group's drummer – at the time of *God Save the Queen*, the controversial single that came out in 1977, the year of Elizabeth II's Silver Jubilee. In the same year, Paul Simonon, bass-player of the Clash, wore the British flag sewn onto his shirt, as the photograph by Kate Simon utilized for the cover of their first album *The Clash* shows.

Punk altered the Union Jack by mixing it up with a contradictory political symbology that comprised Celtic crosses, Japanese military insignia, Nazi eagles and tributes to Italian and German terrorist organizations of the Far Left, such as the T-shirt inscribed with the words 'brigade rosse' and the star of the R.A.F. (Rote Armee Fraktion) worn by Joe Strummer of the Clash at the end of the seventies. Accompanied by the word Destroy, the swastika of the Nazi flag appeared on the T-shirts designed by Malcolm McLaren (manager of the Sex Pistols) and his then companion Vivienne Westwood, at a time when their shop on King's Road in London was one of the principal centres for the development and diffusion of punk aesthetics. Opened in 1971, the shop changed name several times, becoming SEX from 1974, during the punk phase, and Seditionaries ('Clothes for Heroes') from 1976, the period of the Destroy look. Interpretation of punk political symbology has always been problematic, as Roger Sabin points out, going beyond the official character of its antiracist image to look at its repressed history as well: the obsession with the Third Reich of Ian Curtis, the singer of Joy Division; the avowed Neo-Fascist tendencies of groups like

Sham 69 and Skrewdriver, but also the anti-Hispanic sentiments of
Adam and the Ants in the song *Puerto Rican*; the continual references
to the white race on the part of the Clash and the dual face of the
Union Jack, an insurrection against the pervasiveness of American
culture but also symbol of the National Front, the most important
Far Right party in Britain.[10]

Equally complex appears the artistic interpretation of punk, which
had emerged out of British art schools in the years of student protest
and Situationist culture. McLaren, Westwood and Reid all belonged
to the Situationist group King Mob, 'which at its best moment,'
explains Alberto Piccinini, 'had a membership of about sixty, ranging
from sophisticated artists and intellectuals to savage skinheads'.[11] The
forms of appropriation of national, political and military emblems
developed by punk aesthetics drew on the artistic legacy of the Soviet
avant-garde movements, John Heartfield's political photomontages,
Dada nihilism, the Pop celebration of the stereotype and the myth of
the subversive artist, capable of coming up with tactics to get round
the rules of the system. In the seventies, the media amplified and
helped to historicize an image of punk as pure contempt for all
musical and sartorial norms. An interpretation that was shared in
those days by the theorist Dick Hebdige in his fundamental
Subcultures. The Meaning of Style[12] of 1979, although he subsequently
retracted that analysis, branding it too simplistic and explaining,
instead, that 'the visual and musical hyperboles of punk helped the
English fashion industry to prosper'.[13]

In art and fashion, therefore, the cartography of flags that made up a
substantial part of punk imagery remained poised between visions of
refined innovation and commercial success, between nationalism and
anarchy, racism and antiracism. National and military symbology
persisted in the eighties with the success of brands like Boy London
and its provocative association of British identity, swastikas and
Arian eagles. Passing through the references to the Union Jack by

Debbi, Siouxsie and Steve Severin

Siouxsie Sioux with Nazi armband. Photo by Ray Stevenson,
from Nils Stevenson, *Vacant: A Diary of the Punk Years
1976-79*, Thames and Hudson, London 1999

Vivienne Westwood, John Galliano and Alexander McQueen, we come to Desiree Mejer and her label Fake London, where the flag has become a motif of constant reflection. In the summer 2002 collection, for example, the national flag appeared in a chaotic collage of Soviet hammers, glittering flashes, dollars and skulls of the pirate flag. After having been a symbol of British fashion with a transgressive identity for thirty years, in 2005 the Union Jack appeared among crosses and chains on the dresses and accessories of *Pretty N' Punk*, the new series of Bratz dolls known as 'the girls with a passion for fashion!'. In January of the same year, while Queen Elizabeth II of England was engaged in the initiatives to commemorate the sixtieth anniversary of the liberation of the concentration camp at Auschwitz, her nephew, Prince Harry, turned up at a party wearing a red band with a swastika on his arm along with the uniform of General Erwin Rommel's Afrika Korps.[14] This shocking gesture by the third in line to the English throne shows that today fashion and art are not the only ones to adopt the logic of appropriation by drawing on the political repertoire of flags. The fashion magazine *Tank* suggests that politics can take its inspiration from fashion and design, imagining playfully that its own name and logo should be adopted by the flags of the Ukrainian political movement of the Orange Revolution.[15] The pun is based on the extraordinary graphic resemblance between the magazine's name and the slogan 'Tak!' ('Yes!' in English) that appeared on the flags displayed by the crowds of Ukrainian demonstrators in the photograph by Gleb Garanich published in *Tank* in February 2005.

NOTES_____

[7] Cf. Dilys E. Blum, *Shocking! The Art and Fashion of Elsa Schiaparelli*, Philadelphia Museum of Art-Yale University Press, Philadelphia-New Haven 2003, p. 205.

[8] Angela Carter, '1967: Notes for a Theory of the Sixties Style', in *New Society*, 1967, then id., *Nothing Sacred*, Virago, London 1982. The passage has been translated from the Italian version, in Paola Colaiacomo, Vittoria C. Caratozzolo (eds.), *Mercanti di stile. Le culture della moda dagli anni '20 a oggi*, Editori Riuniti, Rome 2002, p. 289.

[9] *Ibidem*. The passage has been translated from the Italian version, in Colaiacomo, Caratozzolo (eds.), *Mercanti di stile*, cit.

[10] Roger Sabin, '"I Won't Let That Dago By". Rethinking Punk and Racism', in Roger Sabin (ed.), *Punk Rock: So What? The Cultural Legacy of Punk*, Routledge, London 1999, pp. 199-218.

[11] Alberto Piccinini, 'Demolire la quarta parete del rock', in Giorgio Agamben (et al.), *I Situazionisti*, Manifestolibri, Rome 1991, p. 58.

[12] Cf. Dick Hebdige, *Subcultures. The Meaning of Style*, Methuen & Co., London 1979.

[13] Id., *Hiding in the Light. On Images and Things*, Comedia-Routledge, London 1988. The passage has been translated from the Italian edition, *La lambretta e il videoclip. Cose & consumi dell'immaginario contemporaneo*, EDT, Turin 1991, p. 223.

[14] Harry the Nazi. Prince's swastika outfit at party', in *The Sun*, 13 January 2005, cover.

[15] Masoud Golsorkhi, 'Editor's Letter. The Importance of Being Earnest', in *Tank*, series IV, no. 1, February 2005, p. 16.

STATES OF FASHION

Western Fashion obsessively tots up the number of results achieved
and to be achieved, the lands already conquered and the ones into
which it can still expand its domination. This chapter provides an
opportunity to look at the boundaries of fashion and to reflect on the
flags that it has metaphorically raised in order to defend and promote
its own elective homelands. What interests us here is not the
relationship between global culture and Western fashion – a subject I
intend to tackle in the following chapters – but the way in which the
latter's ubiquity is often paradoxically founded on the enhancement
of local qualities. In this sense flags take part in the discourse of
fashion, which in turn participates in the construction of the image of
entire nations, strengthening the ties between style and national
identity. The time when the French tricolour flew confident and
alone over the realm of fashion, seen as a form of cultural production
on a national base, is over. Today the flags have multiplied, but
without definitively contradicting a system organized into centres of
creativity, style and consumption. Along with Paris and London,

'The black Marseillaise'. Azzedine Alaïa during the last fitting
of the tricolour tunic worn by the American singer Jessie
Norman for the bicentenary of the French Revolution, directed
by Jean-Paul Goude, 14 July 1989. Photo by P. Perrin
© Sygma

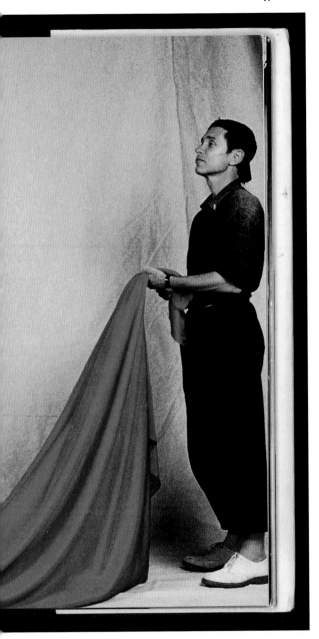

cities like New York, Tokyo, Milan, Antwerp and Amsterdam have been elected capitals of fashion, and some entire nations – such as Italy – its ideal homelands. Yet the majority of these, countries and capitals, are still located along the main axis of the West, between Europe and America, which have founded their cultural hegemony on the ideals of modernity, urbanity and civilization.

In 1940 Christian Dior had not yet become the most famous couturier in France, but was already involved in fashion and illustration. Evidence of this comes from a menu he designed on 2 January, a few months before the German occupation of France during the Second World War. The names of the courses that made up the meal – handwritten in rapid strokes – are truly French, from the royal hors-d'oeuvre of 'Pâté de tête Charles VII' to the dessert 'Savarin Mehunois', perhaps in homage to one of the residences of the king of France, the chateau of Mehun-sur-Yèvre, where Charles VII himself had died in 1461. The nationalism of the menu is underlined by Dior's illustration, but the historical and monarchic references are couched in a modern and republican key. In fact his illustration consists of a bouquet made up of a lily, a daisy and a poppy, with the three flowers bound together by a large tricolour ribbon. In the place of the central bud of each flower, Dior drew a delicate female face surrounded by a 'corolla', in the colours blue, red and white respectively. Seven years later, the same association of woman and flower would become the guiding thread of his celebrated debut collection, entitled *Corolle*. Returning to the drawing of 1940, the floral arrangement follows a scheme of visual interpretation that respects Western rules: from top to bottom, from left to right. Thus the flower at top left is the lily, and it could not be otherwise since blue is the first and most important colour in the French flag, as Michel Pastoureau points out, explaining its political and national meanings historically.[16] It is followed, as is logical, by the white daisy in the middle and the red poppy, at bottom right.

Elsa Schiaparelli, collection with flags of naval units, 1940
Photo by Man Ray, from *Harper's Bazaar*, March 1940

Emilio Pucci, *Palio* collection, 1957

Fifty years later, a similar blend of French gourmandise and fashion was presented in a post-modern key by the British director Peter Greenaway in his film *The Cook, the Thief, His Wife & Her Lover* (1989). Here too the refined menus are in French, just as the 'cook' who produces them is French. Also indisputably French is Jean-Paul Gaultier, the exceptional costume designer of this film: a sumptuous parade of his creations, commencing with the clothes worn by Helen Mirren in the role of the 'wife', Giorgina. But here the feast of French gastronomic and sartorial refinements – noble expressions of European culture – reveals some darker aspects of that same culture: the willingness to resort to violence, the lust for power and the readiness to abuse it, conveyed cinematographically by the figure of the irascible 'husband'. The film is set in London, at the restaurant *Le Hollandais*. Great Britain, France and the Netherlands, the three nations brought together (the producers of the film are also British, French and Dutch) find a common tricolour representation in the scenery. The midnight blue of the outside of the restaurant, the deep red of the dining hall and, as a sort of decompression chamber between the two, the dazzling white of the toilets. Giorgina's clothes change colour from scene to scene, adapting to the colour of the setting and the circumstances. Blue, white and red are the colours of the French flag, used in the film as an icon of European culture, refined, decadent and diseased. The same colours are used in the flags of Great Britain and the Netherlands and it is hard not to connect the names of these nations (including France) to their past as the main European powers, with their imperialist policies, creation of global links, international trade routes and colonial conquests.
The representations of France based on the stereotype of its *drapeau gourmand* provide the cue for extending the reflection to other elective homelands of fashion. Emblematic is the case of Italy, where the desire to give a clear connotation of identity to its fashion – in contrast to the French one – has been a guiding theme ever since the

Alessandra Vaccari

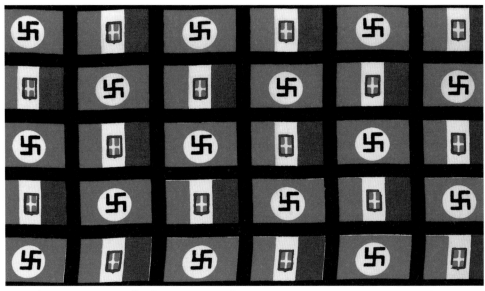

Silk mill in Como, printed taffetas for application, design by
Manlio Rho, 1935-40, Rho Family Archives

19th century, the time of the struggles for the unification of Italy and the choice of the green, white and red tricolour as symbol of the nation. Fashion has often exploited the possibility of embracing the variety of representations of Italy in the simplified and easily identifiable vision of its flag, performing a sometimes promotional and sometimes protectionist function. In the second half of the 1930s, for example, under the Fascist regime, the painter Manlio Rho from Como designed, among other things, propagandistic fabrics for the Italian textile industry. One of these was the taffetas now in the Rho family archives and printed with alternating motifs of Italian and Nazi flags, reflecting the strengthening of ties between Italy and Germany on the plane of dress as well.[17] Nowadays the Italian flag is often utilized in a figurative sense by the world of fashion, showing its pride in 'tricolour brands', 'tricolour products', a 'tricolour flagship store' and 'tricolour successes' in general. At times this is done directly, as in the case of the Roman couturier Valentino who, on the occasion of the presentation of one of his collections of haute couture, projected the image of the Italian flag onto the front of the Parisian branch of his maison, an elegant building facing onto Place Vendôme, the historic heart of French luxury.[18] And the tricolour also became the guiding thread of an exhibition in 2004 that set out to reinforce the link between national identity and a 'made in Italy' now on a collision course with China. *Espressioni di stile sulla bandiera italiana* ('Expressions of Style on the Italian Flag') was the title of this exhibition, organized by the Camera Nazionale di Moda Italiana and staged in Milan, London and Tokyo. To 'the pride of the priests of Made in Italy', declared the press release, 'thirteen celebrated prêt-à-porter labels (Mariella Burani, Roberto Cavalli, Etro, Salvatore Ferragamo, Gattinoni, Iceberg, Gai Mattiolo, Max Mara, Missoni, Anna Molinari per Blumarine, Emilio Pucci, Mila Schön and Trussardi) have each been invited to come up with a personal reappraisal of the national flag'.[19]

In the historical process of building Italy's international reputation as a fatherland of fashion, claims to identity have often played on the tricolour, but it has not been the only factor. Equally important has been the notion of Italy's noble and ancient civilization, seen as the mother of a West which has proclaimed itself the originator of culture and arbiter of fashion: a prejudice that reflects the links between imperialist policies and their symbolic representation. In the twenties and thirties, under the Fascist regime, the effort to create a fashion in the national mould relied obsessively on exaltation of the taste, sophistication and history of Italian art. In an altered political climate, at the end of the Second World War, it was still the motif of the nation's noble artistic and cultural past that went hand in hand with the success of its fashion on international markets and, first of all, the American one. Fashion is a 'magnificent power that belongs to us by ancestral right',[20] declared the journal of the women's organizations of the National Fascist Party in 1933. 'The Italian art of tailoring is ancestral',[21] stated the American edition of *Vogue* in 1952. In the fifties and sixties, these mythicized visions of Italian fashion found confirmation in the photographic services produced to promote it. Models and clothes glide past the backdrop of a picture-postcard Italy – Roman antiquities, façades of Renaissance churches, fountains and baroque palaces – and connect the 'ancestral right' with the country's noble artistic past. In her book on the development of the Italian fashion industry, Nicola White describes *The Fine Italian Hand* of 1946 as one of the first services that the American edition of *Vogue* had devoted to Italy and noted that:

the illustrations were shot in Rome, in palaces and at ancient sites, and fashions by designers such as Galitzine, Gattinoni and Fontana were worn by aristocratic socialites, including Countess Sandra Spalletti and Countess 'Niki' Visconti. The models appeared like ancient statuary in the niches of classical architecture, and the text was loaded with stereotypical generalisations of the Italian people and culture.[22]

Moschino, collage. From Franco Moschino and Lida Castelli,
Moschino X anni di kaos! 1983-1993, Lybra, Milan 1993

Maurizio Cattelan, *Il Bel Paese*, 1995, woollen carpet,
diameter 320 cm

Courtesy Fondazione Sandretto Re Rebaudengo, Turin

The same connections between ancient statues, models and Italian fashion are underlined in the book *Italian Eyes. Italian Fashion Photographs from 1951 to today*. In the opening sequence of images, for example, there is a photograph by Lina Tenca (*Novità*, September 1957) showing a model-statue next to two marble busts inside a gallery with a barrel vault. The gallery resembles a niche by analogy with the picture on the facing page, where a model photographed by Bob Krieger (*Harper's Bazaar Italy*, December 1970) is really inserted into the space of a precious marble recess.[23] The internationalization of Italian fashion has brought a reinforcement of the stereotypes linked to the image of the country. Fashion has even been able to incorporate into its discourse images that emerged together with the influx of tourists to Italy and the outflow of migrants to America. They include images of a beautiful, picturesque and rural Italy juxtaposed with those of Italo-American ghettos and interwoven with countless stories turning on social marginality, espresso and spaghetti, vendettas in the name of honour and organized crime. These representations are active forces that have helped to define the very idea of Italian Style, seen as a construction capable of making a whole constellation of 'high' and 'low' cultural values and positive and negative stereotypes converge around the symbology of the tricolour. Within it coexist, in fact, the good taste inherited from ancient civilization; the sense of a classical elegance; the baroque fondness for decoration; Mediterranean sensuality; the love of everything that is simple, from food to clothing; technical skill and craft traditions; and the industrial model of the family-run concern and the unique character of the manufacturing areas, these last factors connected with the sense of attachment to family and of belonging to a region respectively. Fashion designers have also devoted themselves to an analysis of Italian stereotypes, and one of the most memorable examples of this is represented by the case of Franco Moschino. The Italian flag has been a constant presence in the work of this stylist

Cover of David Bowie's *Earthling*, 1997

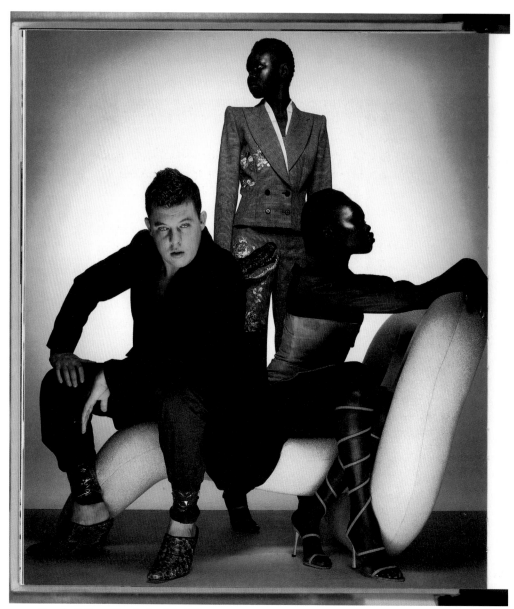

Alexander McQueen. Photo by Sean Ellis, 1997

who between the mid-eighties and the early nineties saturated
collections, catwalks, displays and advertising campaigns with
tricolour visions, reflecting ironically on the image of his country
because, as he has put it, 'pasta and Italy have two things in common:
green and red'.[24] As symbol of a country's identity and style, the flag
also lends itself to telling stories of transit and displacement, as in the
case of the Japanese designer Nigo, creator of the streetstyle label A
Bathing Ape, who in 2004 came out with a line of clothing with the
Italian tricolour and the inscription 'Bape in Italy'.
On the Western scene each 'fatherland of fashion' is assigned a role, a
culture and a coherent set of identifying traits, i.e. a distinctive style,
often encapsulated in the colours of the national flags and called on to
express not just aesthetic but also ethical and economic values. In this
sense people talk of British Style, French Style, Italian Style and so
on, all the way to New Zealand Style, a phenomenon that I intend to
analyze in chapter five.

What fashion does is advertise the city or the country as a whole. So fashion works in
this way, it's about creating an image. This is not unique to Britain, it's exactly what
Armani does on a much bigger scale. His image and his name are exported across the
world – he is Italy.[25]

These words were used by a member of the British Fashion Council
in 1993, during an interview conducted by Angela McRobbie.
While in the middle of the 20th century Italian fashion was still
indebted to its image as the historic homeland of art and culture,
the relationship now seems to have been inverted in favour of fashion
itself, whose representations have repercussions on the national
identity. Commenting on the interview, the British sociologist uses
a gastronomic metaphor and critically points out that in this way
fashion design ends up having the function of 'the icing on the
cake',[26] where the cake is the nation and the icing a shiny and
tempting image of fashion. The formula Armani = Italy is

undoubtedly simplistic and insufficient to capture the more
complicated reality of fashion design. What is certain is, that over the
course of the nineties, the discourse of fashion has made abundant use
of such equations. In a photograph from 1997, for example,
Alexander McQueen is portrayed by Sean Ellis with his eyeballs
covered by Union Jacks. The image proudly flaunts the Britishness of
the young creative director, who has recently been hired by the
French house of Givenchy to replace John Galliano, himself a star of
British fashion design. In the same year as this portrait, the newly
elected prime minister Tony Blair became the political face of 'Cool
Britannia', a campaign of national rebranding devised by the young
policy thinker Mark Leonard with the aim of sprucing up the
country's rather dowdy image. 'Blair is a world leader as nation
stylist',[27] comments the Canadian journalist Naomi Klein in her
bestseller *No Logo* (popular bible of the anti-globalization movement),
explaining that in actual fact it is no longer enough to create an
identification of brand and nation: it has to be done in such a way
that that brand and that nation are perceived as 'cool', keyword of the
nineties and an essential quality for the success of both. On the one
hand a stylist (McQueen) as representative of Britishness in the
world, and on the other a world leader (Blair) as stylist of the United
Kingdom: two opposite but significantly symmetrical visions which
serve to introduce the interactions between fashion, brand and nation,
subject of the next chapter.

NOTES_____

[16] Michel Pastoureau, *Bleau. Histoire d'une couleur*, Seuil, Paris
2000. Eng. trans. *Blue. History of a Color*, Princeton University
Press, Princeton 2001.
[17] Chiara Buss (ed.), *Seta. Il Novecento a Como*, Silvana, Milan
2001, p. 205.
[18] Cf. Susannah Frankel, 'Fashion & Style', in *The Independent*,
17 June 2004.

[19] *Espressioni di stile sulla bandiera italiana*, press release, Camera Nazionale della Moda Italiana, Milan, 17 February 2004.

[20] Enrico Cucci, 'Che cos'è la moda?', in *Il giornale della donna*, yr. XV, no. 6, 15 March 1933, p. 7.

[21] 'Italian Ideas for Any South', in *American Vogue*, November 1951. Translated from the Italian version cited in Guido Vergani, *La Sala Bianca. Nascita della moda italiana*, Electa, Milan 1992, p. 174.

[22] Nicola White, *Reconstructing Italian Fashion. America and the Development of the Italian Fashion Industry*, Berg, Oxford-New York 2000, p. 164.

[23] Maria Luisa Frisa (ed.) with Francesco Bonami and Anna Mattirolo, *Italian Eyes. Italian Fashion Photograph from 1951 to Today*, Charta-Fondazione Pitti Immagine Discovery, Milan-Florence 2005, pp. 20-1.

[24] Franco Moschino and Lida Castelli (eds.), *X anni di kaos! 1983-1993*, Lybra, Milan 1993, p. 297.

[25] Angela McRobbie, *British Fashion Design. Rag Trade or Image Industry?*, Routledge, London-New York 1998, p. 69.

[26] *Ibidem*.

[27] Naomi Klein, *No Logo: Taking Aim at the Brand Name Bullies*, Knopf, Toronto 2000.

UNITED FLAGS OF FASHION

United Colors of Benetton – United States of Australia – United States of Switzerland: the first is the name thought up by Oliviero Toscani for the Italian clothing brand; the second is the slogan of national identity launched by the Australian brand of clothing for surfers Mambo; the third is the ironic outcome of Bruce Mau's seminar on ways of updating the image of Switzerland. The three cases, quite different despite their assonance, do have in common the evocation of the *United States of America* as an unavoidable benchmark of identity. Over the course of the 20th century America, once a colony of Europe and its cultural periphery, has been 'invented after being discovered',[28] as the critic Leslie Fiedler has written, pointing out that the success of this country is the product of negotiations between historical authenticity and stylistic manipulation. Thus America has progressively asserted itself as a promise of wealth and liberty and its Old Glory has become a planet-wide icon of modernity, democracy, the free market and multiculturalism. The flags with the stars and stripes painted in the mid-fifties by the American artist Jasper Johns

United Colors of Benetton advertising campaign, 1985.
Photo by Oliviero Toscani, from *Oliviero Toscani al muro.
L'arte visiva nella comunicazione pubblicitaria di United Colors of
Benetton*, Leonardo Arte, Milan 1999

Medicom Toys, *Devilock Palmboy Kubrick*, 2004. Photo Carlo Fei

bear witness to the fact that they have long become a mirror of global culture. In this chapter I will take a look at this condition, focusing above all on the consequences and contradictions that have emerged in these years of militant attacks on consumer society and no-global resistance. To do this, the three slogans cited at the beginning can serve as points of reference to draw a map of the present conflicts of interest between the flag of the United States and global culture.

It was to the suggestions offered by the flag of the United States that the photographer and art director Oliviero Toscani resorted when, in 1985, he transformed the image and identity of the Italian clothing brand into the ecumenical message *United Colors of Benetton*. At the beginning of his association with Benetton in 1984, the slogan was 'All the Colours of the World'. Abandoning the British English 'colours' in favour of the American English 'colors' reinforced the linguistic parallel between United Colors and United States, as Lorella Pagnucco Salvemini notes in her book.[29] And this correspondence is underlined at a symbolic level, for the word 'colors' is synonymous with the national emblem and, in the jargon of the American navy, refers expressly to the ceremony of saluting the flag. So Toscani was paying a conceptual tribute to the American flag, without needing to insert stars or stripes into the bright green rectangle of the United Colors of Benetton logo. On the one hand this seems to be an invocation of universal brotherhood, mustering all the races and flags of the world; on the other it invites all to wear the Benetton 'colors'. The double meaning is also significantly conveyed through the images of the advertising campaigns conceived by Toscani and based on an idea of universal brotherhood. The campaigns realized between 1984 and 1987, in particular, show blond- and dark-haired youths and black and white children all happily embracing amongst a riot of maps of the world and coloured flags. Yet it is only within the unifying space of the white background and in the presence of the green rectangle of the logo

Nothing succeeds like excess. Photo by David Lachapelle,
fashion editor Patti Wilson, from *L'Uomo Vogue*, no. 347,
January 2004

that these differences are called on to coexist.

Toscani's homage allows us to broaden the discussion and reflect on the way fashion, by setting in motion an endless series of forms of appropriation of the American flag, has played a major part in its transformation into a logo of global culture. Without drawing too many distinctions, this flag has worked its magic for luxury brands as well as those specializing in 'prêt-à-porter', 'streetstyle' and 'pronto moda'. In this sense, Old Glory is truly democratic, always ready to come to the aid even of those who do not have a real brand. A label with the stars and stripes always lends a bit of soul (even if it's fake) to the most anonymous pair of jeans, made in any factory of the First or Third World. A few months ago, I found a denim skirt with a bib, manufactured in Italy in the mid-seventies, on a stall and bought it. Underneath a false pocket on the bib were set two rectangles of applied fabric that evoked the US flag and reinforced the skirt's fictitious foreign identity. It had never been worn and still bore the tag with which it had been put on sale at the time. This was a blue card with the word McAndrew in yellow, the same colours as those of the more famous Wrangler brand. Also interesting was the motto in English set alongside the McAndrew logo, describing it as 'Sixteen Yeors Line', where the reason for the misspelling of the word 'years' became apparent when you looked at the back of the card: 'made in Italy'. The tag can also be regarded as the other side of the coin, throwing light on the pervasive rather than democratic character of American culture. Another example of this is Mambo, an Australian brand of street- and surfwear, and its 'United States of Australia Belt Buckle'. As the name suggests, it is a metal buckle enamelled in the colours and shape of Old Glory, but with the outline of Australia instead of the stars of the federal states of America. This buckle has become one of the symbols of the irreverent twenty years of the brand's history (it was created in 1984) and one of the cult objects most sought-after by collectors of Mambo products. The label has given expression to the feeling of the pervasiveness of American culture and of Australian culture's excessive dependence on it, as is demonstrated by the passage explaining the significance of the 'United States of Australia Belt Buckle':

> Over the past 60 years Australia has maintained what can only be described as a "sluttish" relationship with the US. We've adopted their music, their television, their fashion and in more recent times, their dislike for foreign cultures that aren't Christian, middle class and Anglo-Saxon.[30]

'We live next door to the source of global culture',[31] commented the Canadian designer Bruce Mau, reflecting on the imbalance of power between the United States and Canada at a seminar held in Switzerland which he described in his book *Life Style*. On that occasion, Mau proposed that the people attending the seminar rethink the national identity of Switzerland on the basis of a number of metaphors, including imagining Switzerland as an archive, an entrepreneur and a new entertainment product. The group of participants given the task of thinking of the country as a 'leading-edge think tank' proposed the expression *The United States of Switzerland*. The definition might seem faintly ridiculous, when you compare the central cultural role of the United States with the isolated one of Switzerland, the vast extent of the federal states of American with the small size of the Swiss cantons, the aggressive interventionism of the former with the historic neutrality of the latter and so on. To underline the contrast, Mau illustrated his account of the seminar with an old advertisement for Switzerland, a photograph that epitomized the country's life style in a stereotyped way: two smiling men wearing diamond-pattern sweaters seated at a table spread with enormous tankards of beer and plates of fondue. Around them nothing but snow-clad mountains and, in the upper right-hand corner, the square with a white cross on a red ground of the Swiss flag. Alright, there is a difference between Switzerland and the

United States, but the fascinating square flag of Switzerland has now become a trademark for brands of international fame like Tissot and Swatch, no less than the stars and stripes of the US have for Polo Ralph Lauren, Tommy Hilfiger and, earlier still, Converse, 'America's Original Sports Company', whose 'Chuck Taylor All Star basketball sneakers' of 1923 have become one of the best-known symbols of American culture in the world, with 750,000,000 pairs sold in 123 countries.[32]

In these years of anti-globalization movements and protests against the culture of consumption, the US flag has often been linked with the worldwide expansion of clothing brands and their idolization. What is new is not the link between brand and nation in itself – it is as old as the history of nation states – but the idea that the power exercised by commercial empires and multinationals can be represented through the ambiguous promiscuity of logos and flags. A comparison between two films like *Rollerball* (the version directed by Norman Jewison in 1975) and *The Corporation* of 2003 illustrates this change of perspective well. Both films present a vision of a planet ruled by corporations that control not just the world economy but also the existence and tastes of its inhabitants. *Rollerball* is set in a hypothetical 2018 and describes the struggle of an individual against the rules laid down by the corporations. The film hinges on the violence that the corporations have eliminated in its institutional aspects, like war, only to promote it, instead, in the guise of entertainment: the brutal and highly popular sport known as rollerball. The 'nature and spectacular rise of the dominant institution of our time'[33] are illustrated in a very different way in the more recent film *The Corporation*, a documentary written by Joel Bakan and directed by Mark Achbar and Jennifer Abbot. Playing on the definition of the corporation as a 'legal person', the film explores its pathologies with the tools of psychiatry, concluding that corporations act to all intents and purposes like psychopaths, i.e. they

Tommy Hilfiger advertising campaign, *Family Reunion*,
spring/summer collection 2005

Adbusters, *Guastatori di pubblicità*, invitation to
exhibition/installation, ex Stazione Leopolda, Florence,
6-16 November 2002

Double-page spreads, in *Vogue Italy*, December 1992 and
February 1989. From *DP. Doppie pagine di Anna Piaggi
in Vogue*, Leonardo Arte, Milan 1998

are not responsible for their own actions, and are therefore dangerous. This individualized vision of corporations is remote from that of *Rollerball*, where their representation was entrusted to the anonymity of aseptic control rooms and the inexpressive faces and dark suits of the powerful. *The Corporation*, on the contrary, focuses chiefly on the logo, i.e. on the best-known graphic 'face' of the 'dominant institutions of the planet'. Thus images of Kellogg's, McDonald's, Benetton, Nike, Swatch, Burger King and WB run right through the film in the form of luminous signs, shopping streets, urban landscapes and advertising spots.

Activism against contemporary consumer culture has devoted a great deal of attention to the stars and stripes, seen at times as a mirror of globalization and therefore as a fatal point of reference for the whole world, and at others as an expression of the decline in the sense of national identity, overwhelmed by the bad conscience of commercial brands that have substituted their own emblems for those of the country. The unhealthy relationship between brand and nation is also the subject of the *Corporate US Flag*, a reworking of Old Glory in which the white stars on a blue ground are replaced by logos, including those of Camel, Coca-Cola, Exxon, IBM, Lilly, Mac, McDonald's, Microsoft, Pizza Hut, Shell and Playboy.

The corporate flag of no-global inspiration is the symbol of the campaign *Unbrandamerica*, launched by Kalle Lasn, guru of the movement to subvert advertising and creator of the concept of 'culture jamming' and the magazine *Adbusters* that is its mouthpiece. For *Unbrandamerica* in 2004, which was held on 4 July, the day of American independence, the corporate flag was featured in a full-page advertisement in *The New York Times*, accompanied by the following declaration, which imitates the formula of the pledge of allegiance to the flag:

This July 4th
Because my country has sold its soul to corporate power
Because consumerism has become our new religion
Because a small group of neocons has hijacked our national agenda
and because we've forgotten the true meaning of freedom
The pledge to do my duty and take my country back.[34]

There is something nostalgic about this text, which is interesting because it highlights the way that the message of the anti-consumerism and no-global movements has established a connection between commercial brands and national flags, playing above all on the link between being disillusioned citizens and deluded consumers. In this sense, the virtual equivalence between the idolization of commercial brands and devotion to the flag is proposed as a mirror of the ever weaker identity of individual citizens-consumers swallowed up in a large nation-company.

One of the numerous converts to the philosophy of culture jamming promoted by Lasn is the fashion designer JJ Hudson, creator of the British brand Noki.[35] The name of the brand comes from the word 'icon' (spelled backwards) with the 'c' replaced by 'k', a habitual gesture for the ketamine generation as Joanna Schlenzka explains in her presentation of Noki's case in the magazine called *Another Magazine*.[36] To mass consumption and the spectacular fashion industry, Noki contrasts a work of 'art branding', which consists in the creation of one-off pieces by the customization of second-hand garments and old T-shirts with logos and cartoon characters. A Noki blouse from the spring-summer collection of 2005 is something halfway between the *Corporate US Flag* and the stars-and-stripes flags painted by Ronnie Cutrone with the heroes of Walt Disney and Warner Bros. One of the arresting sleeves of this blouse has red and white stripes, the other white stars on a blue ground. The bodice on the other hand is made up of the remains of a white Diet Pepsi shirt – the red and blue logo still recognizable despite the scissor cuts –

per
Nol
nig

Nol
the
up
of
eve
par
"fr

STYLING **NICOLA FORMICHETTI** HAIR **PAUL HANLON** AT **JULIAN WATSON AGENCY** MAKE-UP **ALEX BOX** AT **HOLY COW** PHOTOGRAPHY ASSISTANT **EMMA ENGQVIST** STYLING ASSISTANTS **CELESTINE COONEY** AND **GARETH EDWARDS** MODEL **DOROTA** AT **SELECT**. FOR MORE INFORMATION CONTACT CUBE PR ON +44 20 7242 5483

Joanna Schlenzka, *Another Corporate Assault*. Photo by
William Selden, styling by Nicola Formichetti, in *Another
Magazine*, no. 8, spring/summer 2005

names, just descriptive monikers – Sporty Spice, Ginger Spice, Scary Spice, Posh Spice and

Spice Girls, 1990s, from Joshua Sims, *Rock Fashion*,
Omnibus Press, London 1999

Bellezza stile liberation. Rosso blu bianco. Photo Chris
Von Wangenheim, from *Vogue Italia*, no. 236, May 1971

Lynda Carter in the TV serial *Wonder Woman*, USA 1976
© Photos12/Grazia Neri

American Defence Secretary Donald Rumsfeld laughing with
Spiderman and Captain America. Photo by Jason Reed
© JASON REED/Reuters/Corbis/Contrasto

Ronnie Cutrone, *Rebellion*, 1991, acrylic on flag, 90 × 170 cm

superimposed on a second shirt with Donald Duck and the word 'Power'. Since the flag of the United States is no longer a promise of freedom, it is used in an attitude of disenchantment, as in the paradoxical case of the Noki brand, which has won itself international recognizability by short-circuiting the stars and stripes and the brands of other companies. But even when companies turn to it with pride, they now do so in an increasingly circumstantial manner, taking care to explain which are the values they want go on being identified with and which they do not. This is the case, for example, with American Apparel, a Californian manufacturer of T-shirts. Concerned about the effects of globalization and environmental and racial questions in particular, American Apparel sets out to restore dignity to its own workers and the activity of manufacturing. It claims to produce 100% of its T-shirts directly, thereby avoiding the dangers of exploitation inherent in the delocalization of clothing manufacture. Demonstrating that in its case the globalization of production has not been an obligatory choice, it goes so far as define itself as 'a capitalist success as much as a socialist success'.[37] Given the company's ethical commitment and name, the confrontation with the symbology of the stars and stripes is inevitable. So it is no accident that an American flag opens the photographic service by Richard Edsen devoted to the company which appeared in the first issue of *The Freshjive Propagandist*, a biannual publication of the Californian brand of streetwear Freshjive. Realized in a black and white evocative of past glories and positive associations for the American flag, the service is set on the downtown Los Angeles premises of American Apparel and features its machinery, workshops, automatic drink dispensers and above all employees: seamstresses, warehouse staff and pattern makers, Hispanic and non-Hispanic working side by side. The American roots of American Apparel are declared with pride in its detailed 'Mission Statement': 'We are about American values. We believe in the American dream and want to do more for our customers and employees'. The American dream indeed, but with a necessary touch of caution: immediately afterwards the statement makes clear that this is not a case of nationalistic zeal: 'We manufacture in the United States, particularly Southern California, not because we are crazy flag fanatics but because it is the most vibrant T-shirt market in the world and therefore the most efficient place to manufacture our T-shirts'.[38]

NOTES_____

[28] Cited in Hebdige, *Hiding in the Light*, cit. The passage has been translated from the quotation in the Italian edition of Hebdige's book, *La lambretta e il videoclip*, cit., p. 128.

[29] Lorella Pagnucco Salvemini, *Benetton/Toscani. Storia di una avventura*, 1984-2000, Bolis, Azzano San Paolo 2002, p. 31.

[30] www.mambo.com.au/mambo.html

[31] Bruce Mau, *Life Style*, Phaidon, London 2002, p. 286.

[32] www.converse.com/zinside.asp?src=cg

[33] www.thecorporation.com/index.php?page_id=2

[34] 'Unbrandamerica.org', full-page advert in *The New York Times*, 3 July 2004.

[35] www.novamatic.com/noki.htm

[36] Joanna Schlenzka, 'Another Corporate Assault', in *Another Magazine*, no. 8, spring-summer 2005, p. 130.

[37] Dov Charney, 'American Apparel', in *The Freshjive Propagandist*, yr. 1, Rick Klotz & Freshjive, Los Angeles 2005, p. 59.

[38] www.americanapparel.net/presscenter/articles/20040517usnews.html

ИEW THIИGS HΛVE TO HΛPPEИ

Viktor Horsting and Rolf Snoeren, better known by the joint name of
Viktor & Rolf, calmly sipped their tea at the Hotel Ritz in Paris
while talking to journalists about *Americana*, their first collection of
prêt-à-porter for autumn-winter 2000/01. Commenting on this
meeting in the May 2000 issue of *Harper's Bazaar*, William
Middleton noted with how much conviction Rolf had declared 'It's a
new century. New things have to happen'.[39] And they have.
It would be going too far to see this collection dedicated to the flag
of the United States – as its name makes clear – as a premonition of
9/11, but it is true that both the design of the clothes and their
interpretation in the fashion reports of the time would have been
inconceivable after that event. The Dutch duo, who up until then had
been known for the extremism of their conceptual haute couture,
chose to exalt the homogenizing face of fashion at the moment when
their work was about to obtain international diffusion and
commercial success through the formula of prêt-à-porter. Without
celebratory intentions and without critical excesses, therefore, the

American flag was treated as a metaphor for the globalization of fashion and contemporary culture. Consistently with this, the models proposed (including polo-necked T-shirts and trousers with five pockets) and the cotton used to make them were borrowed from the basic formula that has become a global icon of American attire. The sampling of pre-existing elements – motifs and models – represented a factor of continuity with respect to Viktor & Rolf's collections of haute couture. But unlike those, often based on the assembly of incongruent fragments, the development of *Americana* was unusually organic and coherent. Only in the motif of the flag did the propensity for collage and the classification and simultaneous accumulation of different parts, practices that characterize the work of the two fashion designers as Richard Martin and Alistair O'Neill for example have pointed out,[40] seem to return. In fact *Americana* does not reproduce Old Glory in its entirety, but some parts of it, mixed up with the stars of the flag of the American confederate states and the large five-pointed star of the US army. This montage of flags was not composed by Viktor & Rolf themselves but taken from a piece of fabric designed in the sixties, according to an article by André Leon Talley published in *American Vogue*.[41] The reference to the sixties is important as it establishes a direct relationship between *Americana* and the Pop culture of that time, with its unreserved consumerist gratifications and the surrender of art to the culture of consumption. Among the photographic services devoted to this collection the one realized by Stéphane Sednaoui for *The New York Times Magazine* retraces 'the odyssey of going global, symbolized by a flag print from the country with the most commercial culture of all'.[42] In the opening picture of this service, the model Alek Wek is portrayed in the guise of the role played by Peter Fonda in the 1969 film *Easy Rider*: Captain America. Dressed in the stars and stripes, she rides a Harley-Davidson against the infinite horizons of the United States, as if in a remake of that film, where Peter Fonda and Dennis Hopper are

Viktor & Rolf, *Americana* collection, autumn/winter 2000/01,
in *Fashion of the Times*. Photo by Stéphane Sednaoui, styling by
Elisabeth Stewart, from *The New York Times Magazine*, part 2,
fall 2000

Peter Fonda in *Easy Rider*, USA 1969, directed by
Dennis Hopper
© Snap/Grazia Neri

young motorcyclists who believe in the American dream and in the apotheosis of freedom but in the end are crushed by them.

The success of Viktor & Rolf's collection can be gauged through its translation into ready-to-wear, which immediately took up and set its seal of approval on *Americana*, translating the motif of the collage of flags into an endless series of T-shirts, shirts, ties and trousers. All this before 11 September and 8 October 2001, when the German group Escada inaugurated the 3000 meters of its new flagship store on Fifth Avenue, decorating it entirely with stars and stripes. Stores like Bergdorf Goodman, Burberry, Hugo Boss, Lord and Taylor, Louis Vuitton and Versace, among others, have followed the same example in New York, while the Chase Manhattan Bank has even been wrapped from head to foot with the flag of the United States. But in Escada's case, in addition to an expression of grief for the tragic event, the red, white and blue fitting-out of the shop functioned as an anticipation of the womenswear line for spring 2002, dedicated to the same flag.

Fashion, flags and business: I don't think it is irreverent to refer to the consequences of 11 September in this way. This trio, in fact, has also provided the basis for Fashion for America, the national campaign of support for the families of the victims of the World Trade Center, organized by the CFDA (Council of Fashion Designers of America) in collaboration with the magazine *Vogue*. 'Shop to show your support' was the slogan of the campaign launched by the then mayor Rudolph Giuliani at the press conference held in New York on 23 October 2001. Giuliani was flanked by the model Carolyn Murphy and the fashion designers Donna Karan and Ralph Lauren, the very symbols of American fashion. Each of them was wearing the T-shirt with a red, white and blue 'mended heart' designed for the occasion by Peter Arnell and produced in a limited run to raise money. Sales of this T-shirt brought over one million and six hundred thousand dollars into the Twin Towers Fund.[43]

DKNY advertising campaign, spring/summer collection 2002,
photo by Peter Lindbergh, creative director Trey Laird
Brilliant White Polo Paint, Ralph Lauren Home
Giorgio Armani store, New York, post-11 September 2001
Chase Manhattan Bank, New York, post-11 September 2001

Instuctions: Artwork for FRONT of T-shirt. Cut out close to edge of design before ironing.

ZERO TOLERANCE

Instuctions: Artwork for BACK of T-shirt. Cut out close to edge of design before ironing.

Judy Blame, *Zero Tolerance* T-shirt, 2002

Even before providing a testimonial for the *Fashion for America* campaign, Ralph Lauren had identified the combination of fashion, flags and business as the best response to 9/11. On 21 September, again in New York, he opened his pared-down fashion parade with a short speech in which he stressed the need to go on thinking about business even in the face of such a tragedy. For the occasion, he wore one of his sweaters with the American flag on the chest, along with a faded pair of jeans and a leather belt. The realism of his speech contrasted with the atmospheres of reverie and romantic escapism conjured up by the collection shown immediately afterwards but, as Bridget Foley pointed out in an article in the *WWD*, the power of the world created by Lauren lies mainly in this contradiction: 'The combination of mythic possibility and business brilliance has made Lauren indisputably the most successful designer in the history of American fashion'.[44] Frequenting the repertoires of country, western and casual, he has created a commercial empire that had an estimated global turnover of ten billion dollars in 2002.[45] In this career his identification with the history and myths of the country has been total since 1967, when he started to present himself as the first American stylist to design clothes for Americans (or for those who wanted to feel American). But his direct recourse to the imagery of the flag is more recent, dating from 1987, when he began to produce sweaters with the emblem of the stars and stripes. In 1993 he brought out the line Polo Sport, whose label was a stylized version of the same flag that now — with the initials RL instead of stars — appears on the tins of Polo Paint from the Ralph Lauren Home line. What has been said so far demonstrates the important role that the American flag played during the emergency of 11 September, when the financial impact of the disaster took up a great deal of people's energies, in the world of fashion as well as that of politics. In the immediate aftermath manufacturers of flags even derived some benefit, as the art historian Jon Bird has pointed out in an article,

quoting the figure of 116,000 flags sold by Wal-Mart on the day of
the attack on the World Trade Center alone.[46] In the same article the
author reflects on what sort of image would be capable of providing a
real and symbolic key to visualizing and understanding the trauma of
that moment. He suggests that the dominant visual trope of 11
September is the cloud of dust generated by the implosion of the
Twin Towers.

If the iconic image of an uncertain post-war world is the mushroom cloud (which, like the
repressed, seems always to return), then the visual legacy of 9/11, surely, is 'dust'. It even has its
own human symbol in 'the Dust Lady' – Marcy Borders – whose shrouded figure emerging
from the rubble was reproduced across much of the visual documentation of the day. *The
Guardian* (3 September 2002) mentions a flyer taped to a lamp-post in Battery Park requesting
participants for a study into the 'post-9/11 exposure to dust', and describes the display in the
window of Chelsea Jeans on Broadway, 'where a rack of denims and sweatshirts still stands,
thickly crusted with yellow dust, frozen in time within a glass cabinet'.[47]

If the pure colours and sharp geometries of an overexposed American
flag are the official image of post-11 September, its counter-image is
the blurred vision of the fine, thick and toxic dust into which the
World Trade Center, and the people and data contained in it, were
vaporized. Broadening the discussion from the traces of the impact to
its aesthetic repercussions, Bird describes the forms in which these
traces have been sublimated in design and in clothing, where there
was immediately talk of a new comfort, of cocoons to increase
people's sense of security, of sharp lines that would give their wearers
the impression of being able to escape quicker and of stratagems to
counter the anxieties of daily life.

In confirmation of this interpretation, I think it is useful to recall the
case of the emerging fashion designer Karen Walker from New
Zealand and her post-9/11 collection, presented in London in the
spring of 2002. Significantly entitled *Dust*, the collection used
subdued colours and hand-knitted wool, conveying a sense of comfort
at the same time as stirring idyllic memories of childhood. In an

Justin Timberlake. Photo by Steven Klein, styling by
Karl Templer, from 'Justin sync', in *Arena Homme plus*,
autumn/winter 2001/02, no. 16

article published in the Observer Magazine under the title *Comfort and Joy*, Walker explained that the collection was suited to the new mood in fashion, given that 'In Europe and America, partly because of September 11th and the state of the economy, there's a move towards dressing down, which is what we're about'.[48]

On the theme of flags, Karen Walker and the New Zealand fashion-design scene now deserve wider consideration, with a view to showing the important role played by fashion in actions of national rebranding. It is only since the end of the nineties that the name of New Zealand has made its way onto the international fashion circuit. Here it has begun to be celebrated for its distinctive and cutting-edge style, often defined as 'intellectual', 'nostalgic', 'edgy' and 'dark', to quote the analysis of the New Zealand academic Maureen Molloy.[49] The history of the emergence of this unexpected creative phenomenon is comprised within a handful of years and names, including those of Nom D', Karen Walker, World and Zambesi, otherwise known as the 'New Zealand Four', a collective label under which they were presented at the London Fashion Week in February 1999. A label that is highly reminiscent of the 'Antwerp Six' (Dirk Bikkembergs, Ann Demeulemeester, Walter Van Beirendonck, Dries Van Noten, Dirk Van Saene and Marina Yee), coined in 1986 on the occasion of another London Fashion Week. The resemblance is not accidental as it is now widely held that the fashion designers of New Zealand today are as innovative, conceptual and profound as their Belgian colleagues were in the nineties. Following the course suggested by the Belgians, and by the Dutchmen Viktor & Rolf, the creation of the fashion image of the New Zealanders has to some extent gone through the same phases, moving from the art circuit to the commercial one: from exhibitions in galleries to fashion shows, from the entrance of their creations into museum collections to their appearance in stores attentive to new trends, including Colette in Paris, b-store and Euphoria in London, Barneys in New York and

Joyce in Hong Kong.

The promotion of New Zealand fashion design on an international scale prompts at least a couple of reflections. In the first place, it is interesting to note how over the last twenty years the uninterrupted and laborious promotion of entire nations in terms of fashion has frequently focused on places that are not easily identifiable with the image of havens of the creative avant-garde. The conjuring tricks and magic powers of fashion. Fashion does not just work on national identities with the aim of reinforcing them, as I showed in chapter three, but is also capable of manipulating them in an unexpected way, distorting them and making them more attractive. I am thinking, for example, of the case of Japan and the way its image as a voracious and devoted consumer of Western labels has been transformed, over the last decade, into a new mecca of young tendencies and street fashion. The same is true for Belgium, whose notorious insensitivity to the delights of the table (epitomized by the national dish of *moules et frites*) and dress (grey or beige mackintoshes, summer and winter) has been turned, 'through an iron will', into an alluring icon of 'austerity', 'rigour' and 'radicalism'. I have taken the definitions in inverted commas from an article by Cédric Saint-André Perrin and Paquita Paquin that appeared in Beaux Arts Magazine in 2000.[50] The emergence of a New Zealand with a creative face is provoking a thorough reinvention of the whole country, identified until just a few years ago with the slogans of the 'clean and green nation' or the 'permanent-press polyester paradise'.[51] But there is more, and this is where we come to the second reflection. The operation of rebranding New Zealand has directly involved the country's flag, since a movement of opinion that has spread to the national level has proposed that it be changed. Given that New Zealand is part of the Commonwealth, the upper left quarter of its flag is still occupied by the Union Jack of Great Britain, and this blatantly reflects its colonial legacy, as well as making it easy to

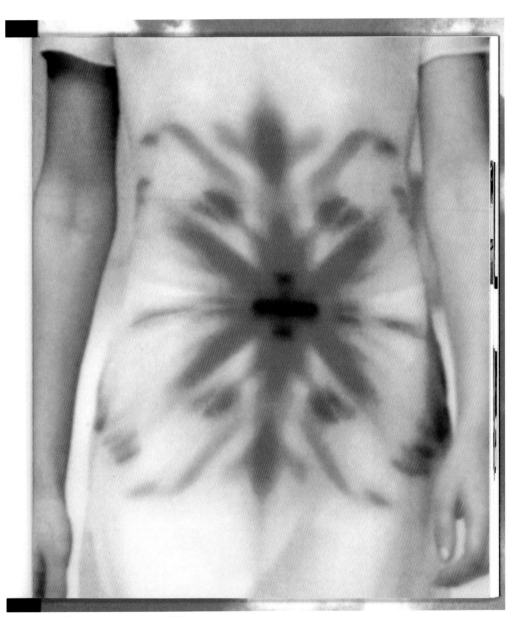

Scott Crolla, spring/summer collection 1997

Stefano Cagol, *1000 mini flags + 1 girl + 1 mini dress +1 flag*,
performance, 1 June 2005, Opening of the 51st International
Exhibition of Art, Venice
Courtesy Stefano Cagol-Galleria Oredaria, Rome

confuse with other, similar flags, commencing with the Australian one. According to the promoters of the campaign for the abolition of the old flag, the new one ought to be capable of visually expressing the complexity of a country in which Maori, Polynesian, European and Asiatic cultural heritages all come together. By adopting a more distinctive and seductive design, it would also be able to represent the rapid modernization carried out by the government in recent years, with the liberalization of foreign trade and an increase in investment on behalf of cultural and creative industries. Significantly, one of these is fashion, which government policy now sees as a strategic area for promoting the economic growth of the nation along with its new image. In this operation the flag assumes the role of a national logo, and this is openly declared on the website of the organization that coordinates the debate over the question. 'As an export country competing on the world stage, we need our flag to be strongly competitive from a brand/symbol/icon point of view'.[52] On the same site Karen Walker expresses her own opinion, saying that 'The current New Zealand flag is irrelevant and unidentifiable. It's not a flag to build a future on.'[53] The statement offers an insight into the role of fashion in this act of national rebranding. Understood as a process of shaping the self and the world, fashion creates identities rather than inheriting them passively and shows how important it is to capitalize the future, and not just history and the past. All this is evident in the case of the new scene in New Zealand, New Zealand, where fashion elaborates the old sense of cultural inferiority towards Europe. New Zealand fashion designers openly include Western references in their 'Southern' collections instead of disowning them, and show that in fashion cultural identity is not always a set condition, but can also be a promise, like the colours and design proposed for the future flag: a stylized white fern on a black ground. There is the nation and there is the imagi-nation, suggests the British historian Theodore Zeldin in this connection, in his *Manifesto* for the fashion magazine ...*and?*:

The nation is what we have inherited and it is what we are born with, and the imagi-Nation is
where we construct ourselves. We have to live with the two. Not everybody, however, wishes to
live in imagi-Nation. Indeed, the majority do not, because it's easier to live in routine and it's
safer to do what is expected of you. [...] The question therefore is: how do you have dialogue
between the nation and the imagi-Nation?[54]

NOTES_____

[39] William Middleton, 'New Amsterdam. Dutch design team
Viktor & Rolf scores an international hit with its first collection
of flag-waving ready-to-wear', in *Harper's Bazaar*, May 2000,
p. 191-194, now in *ABCDE Magazine: Viktor&Rolf par Viktor
et Rolf*, première décennie, 2003, p. 155-158.
[40] Richard Martin, Viktor & Rolf, *Le regard noir*, no. 28,
www.smba.nl/shows/28/28.htm. Text of the exhibition at the
Stedelijk Museum in Amsterdam, 5 April-18 May 1997, later
expanded in Richard Martin, 'A Note: Art & Fashion, Viktor &
Rolf', in *Fashion Theory*, yr. 3, no. 1, March 1999, pp. 109-20.
Alistair O'Neill, *Cuttings and Pastings*, in Christopher Breward
and Caroline Evans (eds.), *Fashion and Modernity*, Berg,
Oxford-New York 2005, pp. 175-89.
[41] André Leon Talley, 'The Flag Bearers', in *American Vogue*,
May 2000, p. 150, now in *ABCDE Magazine*, cit., p. 159.
[42] 'Fashion of the Times', in *The New York Time Magazine*,
part II, fall 2000, now in *ABCDE Magazine*, cit., p. 133.
[43] *Fashion for America*, www.cfda.com/flash.html
[44] Bridget Foley, 'The Importance of Being Ralph', in *WWD*,
section II, 14 May 2002, p. 4.
[45] polo.com/history/history.asp?year=2002
[46] Jon Bird, 'The mote in God's eye: 9/11, then and now',
in *Journal of Visual Culture*, yr. II, no. 1, April 2003, p. 85.
[47] *Ibidem*, p. 91.
[48] Tamsin Blanchard, 'Comfort and Joy', in *The Observer
Magazine*, 25 August 2002,
shopping.guardian.co.uk/clothes/story/0,1586,780243,00.html
[49] Cf. Maureen Molloy, 'Cutting-edge Nostalgia: New Zealand
Fashion Design at the New Millennium', in *Fashion Theory*,

yr. 8, no. 4, November 2004, pp. 477-90.

[50] Cédric Saint-André Perrin and Paquita Paquin, 'La mode en capitales', in *Beaux Arts Magazine*, special issue *Qu'est-ce que la mode aujourd'hui?*, 2000, pp. 26-33.

[51] The slogans are cited in Alison L. Goodrum, 'The First New Zealand Fashion Week Exhibition', in *Fashion Theory*, yr. 8, no. 1, February 2004, pp. 101-2.

[52] Brian Sweeney, *Eight Reasons to Change the New Zealand Flag*, www.nzflag.com/essay_sweeney.cfm, February 2004.

[53] Statement by Karen Walker, at www.nzflag.com/endorsements.cfm?i=46

[54] Theodore Zeldin, 'A Manifesto for ...and?', in *...and?*, March 2002.

ИО МАИ'S LAИD

In the previous chapters I have concentrated my attention on the
flags of nation states in order to assess their role as maps of visual
identity; the characteristic of distinctive design; the stereotyped
appearance; the ability to transform that appearance in part through
fashion; the often ambiguous relationships that they maintain with
commercial brands; and finally the reasons why certain flags, like that
of the United States, have become models of style and others not.
Thus I have looked at the American, French, Japanese, Indian,
Italian, Palestinian, New Zealand, German and Vatican flags, among
others. Many are still unaccounted for, even if we limit our attention
to the ones that appear most frequently in our wardrobes. Missing,
for example, are the national colours of Jamaica, Cuba, Korea, China
and Brazil, the last of which have for some time now become the
constant chromatic backdrop to our summers.

Flags are not just a symbol of the identity and style of the nations
they represent, but also serve to highlight migrations of geography
and environment. The present cultural and racial complexity of the

Antonio Marras, autumn/winter collection 2005/06

Sislej Xhafa, *Clandestine Pavilion*, 1997, performance at the
47th International Exhibition of Arts, Venice, photograph,
160 × 110 cm
Courtesy Sislej Xhafa - Magazzino d'Arte Moderna, Rome

Chiri, spring/summer collection 2005

United Kingdom inspired the *Reflag* campaign conceived by Nigel Turner in 2003 with the aim of enriching the white, red and blue pattern of the Union Jack by inserting a bit of black.[55] With this proposal Turner hopes to free the British flag from its racist associations since, as he explains, 'if I flew the union jack from a flagpole in my garden, many people would see it as a racist statement'.[56] Such associations are deeply stamped on this national flag: from the times when Great Britain was the major colonial power of the West to the 1970s and 1980s, when skinheads and supporters of the England football team used to sing the refrain 'There ain't no black in the Union Jack, send the bastards back!'[57]

The addition of a colour, however emblematic, is perhaps not sufficient to represent a process of broader scope that has to do with globalization and the delicate relations between questions of identity and experiences of uprooting. A fixed point of the cultural criticism that deals with such processes is the conviction that racial, cultural and visual identities are less and less bound to the coherent and organic image of a nation. As products of history, the nation states are not eternal and are no longer – if they ever were in the past – homogeneous representations of the idea of homeland, citizenship and membership of a community. The power of national flags seems to wane for those who, for example, identify simultaneously with more than one nation: the one they were born in, the one their family comes from and the one they have chosen to live in. As I head towards a conclusion, I would now like to consider the ability of transnational and diasporan flags to represent divided, multiple or hybrid identities. So this chapter is going to focus on the flags of promised and longed-for lands, the flags of those do not want to have a homeland and the utopian ones that symbolize lands which belong to nobody – *no man's lands* – or to everybody.

Red, gold and green are the three colours of the national flag of Ethiopia, but they are also the symbol of Rastafarianism and of a

May Day! May Day!. Photo by Txema Yeste, styling by Miguel
Arnau, from *Collezioni Uomo*, no. 50, spring/summer 2005

mythical homeland to which Rastas yearn to return. Brought to worldwide attention by Jamaican reggae music, Rastafarianism is a religious, political and cultural movement born in Jamaica in the 1920s. The name derives from Ras Tafari Makonnen, who in November 1930 was crowned emperor of Ethiopia under the name Haile Selassie ("Might of the Trinity"). The Rastafarians regard Haile Selassie as an incarnation of God (*Jah*), and thus the highest spiritual as well as political authority for the Afro-Caribbeans of Jamaica, which in the thirties was still under British colonial rule. The fate of the emperor of Ethiopia, who spent the years of the Italian occupation of Ethiopia in exile in England, also helped to feed the myth of the diaspora. In fact the existential condition of exile is something the people of Africa have in common: from the painful memory of slavery to the mass migrations to the West. The Rastafarian alternative to the Western model takes the form of a coherent culture that is a syncretic fusion of religion, music and specific styles of life and dress: dreadlocks, crocheted caps and the red, gold and green and lion of Judah of the Ethiopian flag. After the persecution in the 1970s that accompanied the success of reggae music, Rasta culture began to earn widespread appreciation. The British punks, for example, took from it both the rhythms of reggae and the Rastafarian contempt for Babylonia (Western civilization founded on exploitation and White dominance). With the growing attention paid in the West to street culture and styles, the interest in the world of Rasta grew as well, and this was reflected in the first wave of fake dreadlocks like those worn by Boy George in the eighties. In discussions of streetstyle, the spread of this interest has often been contrasted with the originality, purity and profundity of Rasta culture, which makes any reworking in fashion terms seem to take on the character of a misappropriation, if not downright profanation. An example of this is offered by Ted Polhemus who, in his influential book *Street Style*, has the following to say about Boy George's choice:

its effect was to take a style which had originally served as a visual expression of religious belief and remove from it all meaning except 'I'm trendy'. In Babylon, the true is made false, the symbolic is made arbitrary and the authentic is made into fashion.[58]

From punk to hip-hop, the Rasta colours have been adopted by streetwear and skatewear brands like Stüssy and Ipath, whose Reed Rasta and Yogi Hi Rasta models of rider footwear openly declare the debt in their names. In 2004 the pop star Gwen Stefani also succumbed to Rasta influences, but transformed the Ethiopian lion of Judah – symbol of the descendants of King Solomon – into a more home-grown lamb of God and adopted the acronym L.A.M.B. (*Love. Angel. Music. Baby*) as the brand for her line of clothing.[59] The red, gold and green tricolour also appeared in Rifat Ozbeck's 1991 spring-summer collection; it is associated with the lion of Judah and a traditional Caribbean repertoire of palms and flowers in the 2005 spring-summer collection of the brand Dsquared2; and finally it characterizes John Richmond's spring-summer collection for 2006, which revives the connection between Rasta and punk. The fashion world's growing interest in the Rastafarian colours becomes undeniable when we find John Galliano designing the Rasta Logo line for Christian Dior. With a nod in the direction of hip-hop culture, Galliano has brought about a collision between a label symbolic of Western luxury and the Rastafarian vision of a diabolically perverse Babylonia. Fashion is transforming the specific cultural and historic character of the Rasta phenomenon into a more easily shared symbol of the contemporary transnational condition, and therefore one that transcends the African diaspora. On the other hand, as the sociologist Paul Gilroy has pointed out, the concept of African diaspora is also changing and the idea of the exodus, which Rastafarianism has borrowed from the Old Testament, seems to have lost a bit of its shine. Gilroy writes, in fact, that 'this identification with the epic of the Exodus and with the story of the chosen people

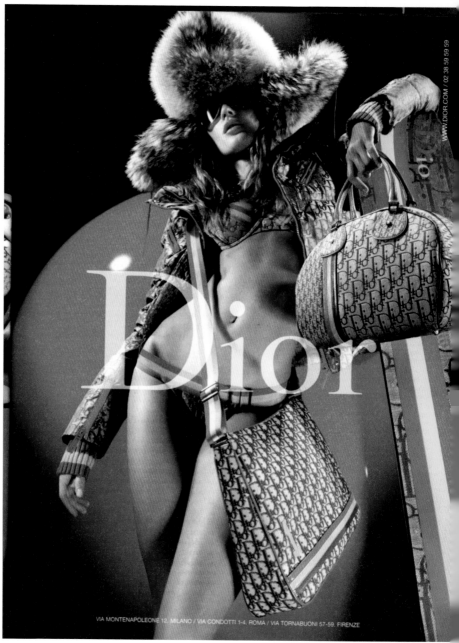

Christian Dior, autumn/winter collection 2004/05

Bob Marley, 1970s, from Carlos Monty, *Bob Marley: Positive Vibration*, La Mascara, Valencia 1995

Prada, spring/summer collection 2005

and their escape from Egypt seems to be in decline. The Black today seem to find it easier to identify with the fascinating pharaohs than with the wretched condition of the people they held in slavery'.[60] Perhaps it is no coincidence that Galliano has dedicated his phantasmagorical 2005 spring-summer collection of haute couture to a mythicized civilization of the Nile Valley, to a seductive, luxurious and gaudily gilded Ancient Egypt.

When black is added to the red, gold and green it is in order to link Rastafarianism to its prophet: the Jamaican political and spiritual leader Marcus Garvey, founder of the pan-African Universal Negro Improvement Association (UNIA) in 1914. The latter's flag – with horizontal red, black and green stripes – is an enduring icon of Afrocentric nationalism: from 'Black liberation' to 'Black power'. Alternating with Rasta gold, its colours appear in the *Freedom One Day* T-shirt (2002) made by the British artist Chris Ofili in collaboration with fashion designer Joe Casely-Hayford. Produced in a limited edition, the T-shirt was shown at the exhibition *Black British Style* held at the Victoria & Albert Museum in London in October 2004. The same combination of Rastafarian and Garveyan iconography appears in the Prada collection for spring-summer 2005. Presented to the rhythm of Jamaican music, the collection of womenswear comprises shawls and sweaters in red, black and green stripes, jewellery and shoes in Rasta colours and the feathers of Caribbean birds. Everyone is familiar with the red, black and green flag, even white people, explained Mau Mau Big Black Africa in Spike Lee's film *Bamboozled* (2000). The film also includes a hilarious parody of fashion designer Tommy Hilfiger, whose brand in the American colours of red, white and blue is transformed into the combination of red, black and green. Hilfiger has often been criticized for the hyper-patriotism of his advertising campaigns, where black and white coexist idyllically beneath the stars and stripes of the inevitable national flag. Despite the apparent racial

Chris Ofili in collaboration with Joe Casely Hayford, *Freedom One Day* T-shirt, 2002, cotton, S M L XL
Courtesy Chris Ofili - Afroco and Victoria Miro Gallery, London

Cover of Bob Marley & the Wailers' *Survival*, 1979

Bamboozled, directed by Spike Lee, produced by Alliance
Atlantic Communication-New Line Cinema, USA 2000

impartiality of such campaigns and the fact that Black rappers like Goldie have worn T-shirts with his brand in big block capitals, Hilfiger's antiracism does not appear to convince the American media. The tide of charges of racism grew so overwhelming that Hilfiger created a section entitled *Rumor* on his website to defend himself.[61] In the film *Bamboozled*, Spike Lee caricatures Hilfiger by creating a part called Hillnigger and giving it to the rapper and political activist Danny Hoch. A group of Black girls and boys dance happily around wearing the clothes of the red, black and green Hilnigger brand, while Hilnigger himself urges them on with this rap:

Yoh! My name be Timmi Hillnigger.
I was born and raised up in Strong Island so you know I know about my peeps, my niggaz in the git-toe. I design and own TIMMI HILLNIGGER 125% Authentic Git-Toe active wear. If you want to keep it really real, never get out of the git-toe, stay broke and continue to add to my multibillion dollar corporation, keep buyin' all my gear. The Timmi Hillnigger collection. We keep it so real we give you the bullet holes.

Another example of a political banner is provided by the extraordinary capacity to create a sense of transnational solidarity possessed by the colour red at the beginning of the 20th century. Red was the colour of Ernesto 'Che' Guevara, who is kept alive through endless reproductions of the fascinating picture – unkempt beard, beret and star – taken in 1960 by the Cuban photographer Alberto Korda. Out of this came the salute 'Hasta siempre, Comandante' at the end of Carlos Puebla's song. From Andy Warhol's silk-screens to the sea of posters, badges and T-shirts, the icon of Che is still an emblem of social justice and nostalgia for the revolutionary spirit. The same fate befell red flags after 1989, when they started to become more and more desirable despite or because they were seen as utopian. The collapse of the Berlin Wall brought the Soviet era to an end forever. From this moment on, the world was swamped with another tide of relics: T-shirts with the hammer and sickle, Cossack hats with the star of the Red Army and badges enamelled with Lenin's profile. Along with red flags, light-blue Trabants and miniature busts of Marx came back into vogue, proudly displayed in the flats and bars of Berlin, amongst couches upholstered in synthetic red leather and wallpaper in gloomy colours. So at the beginning of the twenty-first century, the affectionate and reassuring trend known as *Ostalgie* took the place of the glacial state-organized choreography of huge waving flags, monumental architecture and bombastic shots from below, interpreted in fashion since as far back as the middle of the eighties by the photographs of fashion designer Thierry Mugler. Even those who reject the idea of patriotism cling to flags: from the red and black ones of the anarchists to the evergreen appeal of the Jolly Roger. The white skull and crossbones on a black ground is one of the emblems most frequently worn for the purposes of intimidation: the insignia used by the pilots of warplanes express a scorn for danger while those of the motorcycle gangs of the fifties amplified their menacing appearance. In the unregulated life led by pirates (including hackers) there is always an element of the criminal, but also of the exotic (i.e. alien), as in the sinister and fascinating Captain Herlock: long hair and scarred face, skull hanging around his neck and billowing cape. Plying the cosmic ocean aboard the Arkadia, this space pirate is the hero of the manga created by the Japanese artist Leiji Matsumoto in 1977 and of the subsequent series of cartoons for television. If the pirate is the emblem of a passion for robbery, he is also a victim of the iconographic plunder carried out by fashion, commencing with the pirate collection of Vivienne Westwood and Malcolm McLaren, presented in Paris in March 1981 and an immediate international success. Between ruffles, boots with buckets, gilt buckles, damasks, stripes, gaudy jewellery and long sideburns, in the years of New Romanticism the pirate trend had the flavour of fantastic adventures in the South Seas. Reflecting on the

Red flag with picture of Ernesto Che Guevara taken
by Alberto Korda in 1960

Printed cotton, late 1920s-early 1930s, anonymous designer
Russian Museum, St Petersburg.

Thierry Mugler, July 1988, from Claude Deloffre, *Thierry
Mugler: Fashion, Fetish, Fantasy*, Thames and Hudson, London
1998

image of the pirate presented by some recent films – including Jack Sparrow (Johnny Depp) in Disney's 2003 *Pirates of the Caribbean: the Curse of the Black Pearl* – the critic Melissa Campbell notes that:

These movie pirates are fashion plates – conjuring up romantic images of puffy shirts, parrots, rakish bandannas, gold earrings, three-cornered hats, eyepatches and velvet coats. [...] It seems that in popular culture, piracy is 1 per cent crime and 99 per cent swashbuckling style.[62]

There is no shortage of pirate flags in the systematic reappraisal of the eighties that is currently underway in fashion, where they are exploited for their extraordinary power to stimulate the imagination and their ability to combine escapism and subversion. Examples of this are the juxtaposition of black lace and see-through panels with heavy metal skulls in Alexander McQueen's collection for autumn-winter 2001/02 and the transformation of the ruches of the pirate shirt into bunches of black skulls in the collection for autumn-winter 200506 of the Japanese designer Jun Takahashi, creator of the Undercover brand. The Jolly Roger flies on pale-pink Vans shoes, on the embroidered sequins of Sonia Rykiel and on the sarcastic 'D.i.o.r. Fall Rush 2004' T-shirt designed by Ken Courtney of Ju$t Another Rich Kid. Jasper Goodall's illustrations with one-eyed female pirates wielding large flintlocks are somewhat reminiscent of the Guns N'Roses T-shirts with a skull and crossed pistols. In fact, the most recent development of the pirate trend in fashion is characterized by a revival of the more macabre and vicious graphics of Heavy Metal and Hardcore groups.

When their aim is to represent the complexity of the inhabited world, people resort instead to the image of the mosaic of flags, in a reflection on the absolutism of the concept of universal homeland and a demonstration of the plurality of identity. In art there are, for example, Alighiero Boetti's embroidered collective maps, Yukinori Yanagi's installations of flags constructed out of coloured sand that are doomed to be mixed up by ants carrying sand from one to another

Capitan Harlock, da Leiji Matsumoto, *Capitan Harlock 4*,
November 2001

Just Another Rich Kid, autumn/winter collection 2004/05

Alexander McQueen, autumn/winter collection 2001/02

Undercover, autumn/winter collection 2005/06

and Pascale Marthine Tayou's *Colonie de foulards* (2004) with flags from all over the world. In 2001, commissioned by the European Union to design an icon of the new Europe, the architect Rem Koolhaas used the image of the mosaic of flags to convey the complexity of modern Europe in a graphically levelling way. Among the many designs he came up with, the one that most caught the interest of the media and public opinion was a synthesis of the forty-eight flags of the European states, elongated and squeezed into many coloured stripes resembling a barcode.[63] Proposals for application of the design include identification papers, backdrops for TV newscasts and tattoos on the back of the necks of European citizens. No flag was envisaged among the potential applications, but when the project hit the press and the web it was immediately seen as an unacceptable threat to the circle of gold stars on a blue ground. And while teachers in Europe complained that the 'new flag' was too complicated for children to learn to draw correctly, commentators and critics accused it of reducing the European identity to the impersonal image of a barcode. If the squeezing of national flags into a single band of coloured stripes can give rise to misunderstandings, the attitude changes when the idea of peaceful coexistence is conveyed by rainbow stripes. The rainbow visions used by the psychedelic culture of the sixties to celebrate peace, love and freedom are echoed both in the Rainbow American flag, gay symbol of free love and pride, and in the Flag of Peace. The latter was put up all over Europe in 2002 to convey an openness to diversity of nation, race and gender in response to the Zero Tolerance war on terrorism launched by the United States after 11 September. In addition to emblems of gay pride and peace, the utopian rainbow has resurfaced in a psychedelic key in the advertising campaign of the Eastpak brand for autumn-winter 2004/05, where a community of koala bears celebrates the liberalization of eucalyptus leaves – *Legalize eucalyptus* – while travelling through the woods aboard an old Volkswagen van

Pascale Marthine Tayou, *Colonie de foulards*, 2004, iron, foulards,
flags, 170 × 1100 × 550 cm
Courtesy Galleria Continua, San Gimignano

Alighiero Boetti, *Map*, 1971, tapestry, 117 × 224 cm,
Carlo and Rosella Nesi collection, Florence

Jota Castro, *Mussolini? He never killed anyone. At the most he sent*
people to the border on holiday, 2003, wax, plastic, fabric, European
flag, nails, environmental installation, one-off piece
Courtesy Galleria Massimo Minini, Brescia

Flag of peace, Full Circle Cult of Denim stand. Photo Andrea
Mugnaini, in *Pitti Immagine Uomo*, no. 68, June 2005

Rem Koolhaas, *Europe barcode*, 2002

Rainbow Flag, 2005

Eastpak advertising campaign, *Legalize Eucalyptus*, 2004

Gsus Industries advertising campaign, 2004, from *i-D*, no. 250, December/January 2004/05

Ugo Rondinone, *Dogs days are over*, 1998, neon, glass, translucent sheet, aluminium, installation at the Centre Culturel Suisse, Paris
Courtesy Galerie Eva Presenhuber, Zurich

Paul Smith, *Women's stripe bag*, 1999, design by Maxine Law, art director Alan Aboud

Jean Charles de Castelbajac, rainbow liturgical habits
for the World Youth Day in Paris in July 1997
© Jean-François Campos/Agence VU

decorated with flowers and a rainbow. In 2004, the rainbow also characterized the publicity for the streetwear brand Gsus, set up in Amsterdam in 1993 by Jan Schrijver and Angelique Berkhout. Various messages in an ecumenical tone appear against a background of multicoloured stripes: 'Try to look like a holiday', 'Have sex with someone you love... Masturbate' and 'Sadness causes colour blindness', associated respectively with a smile, a heart and a crown of thorns (which is also the brand's logo).[64] The rainbow, finally, clothes the Catholic world, as in the case of the liturgical dress designed by Jean Charles de Castelbajac and worn by Pope John Paul II and over five thousand churchmen on the occasion of the World Youth Day held in Paris in July 1997.[65] Peace.

NOTES_____

[55] Cf. www.reflag.co.uk/index.htm

[56] BBC News, *Rebranding puts black marks against UK flag*, 11 June 2003, news.bbc.co.uk/1/hi/uk/2981038.stm

[57] Cf. Les Back, Tim Crabbe and John Solomos, '"Lions, Black Skins and Reggae Gyals". Race, Nation and Identity in Football', in *Cultures of Racism in Football. Research project based at Goldsmiths College*, London 1998, now at www.furd.org/onlineresources/lions.html

[58] Ted Polhemus, *Street Style. From Sidewalk to Catwalk*, Thames and Hudson, London-New York 1994, p. 79.

[59] www.l-a-m-b.com

[60] Paul Gilroy, *The Black Atlantic. Modernity and Double-Consciousness*, Verso, London-New York 1993. The passage has been translated from the Italian edition *The Black Atlantic. L'identità nera tra modernità e doppia coscienza*, Meltemi, Rome 2003, p. 338.

[61] www.tommy.com/about/rumor.aspx

[62] Melissa Campbell, 'Pirate chic', in *The Age*, 30 January 2004, www.theage.com.au/articles/2004/01/30/1075340827447.html?from=storyrhs

[63] Amoma, *Rem Koolhaas & Simon Brown, Jon Link, Content.*

Triumph of Realization, Taschen, Cologne-London-Paris 2004, pp. 384-385.

[64] www.g-sus.com/

[65] Florence Müller, *JC de Castelbajac*, Assouline, Paris 2000, p. 78.

BIBLIOGЯΛPHY

American Apparel,
www.americanapparel.net/presscenter/articles/20040517usnews.html

Amoma, Rem Koolhaas & Simon Brown, Jon Link, *Content. Triumph of Realization*,
Taschen, Cologne-London-Paris 2004.

Arjun Appadurai, *Modernity at Large. Cultural Dimensions of Globalization*, University
of Minnesota Press, Minneapolis-London 1996. Italian edition *Modernità in polvere.
Dimensioni culturali della globalizzazione*, Meltemi, Rome 2001.

Les Back, Tim Crabbe and John Solomos, '"Lions, Black Skins and Reggae Gyals".
Race, Nation and Identity in Football', in *Cultures of Racism in Football*. Research
project based at Goldsmiths College, London 1998, now at
www.furd.org/onlineresources/lions.html

BBC News, *Rebranding puts black marks against UK flag*, 11 June 2003,
news.bbc.co.uk/1/hi/uk/2981038.stm

Jon Bird, 'The mote in God's eye: 9/11, then and now', in *Journal of Visual Culture*, yr. II, no. 1, April 2003.

Tamsin Blanchard, 'Comfort and Joy', in *The Observer Magazine*, 25 August 2002, shopping.guardian.co.uk/clothes/story/0,1586,780243,00.html

Dilys E. Blum, *Shocking! The Art and Fashion of Elsa Schiaparelli*, Philadelphia Museum of Art-Yale University Press, Philadelphia-New Haven 2003.

Chiara Buss (ed.), *Seta. Il Novecento a Como*, Silvana, Milan 2001.

Melissa Campbell, 'Pirate chic', in *The Age*, 30 January 2004, www.theage.com.au/articles/2004/01/30/1075340827447.html?from=storyrhs.

Angela Carter, '1967: Notes for a Theory of the Sixties Style', in *New Society*, 1967, then id., *Nothing Sacred*, Virago, London 1982, pp. 85-90. Italian version in Paola Colaiacomo and Vittoria C. Caratozzolo (eds.), *Mercanti di stile. Le culture della moda dagli anni '20 a oggi*, Editori Riuniti, Rome 2002.

Dov Charney, 'American Apparel', in *The Freshjive Propagandist*, yr. 1, Rick Klotz & Freshjive, Los Angeles 2005.

www.converse.com/zinside.asp?src=cg

Enrico Cucci, 'Che cos'è la moda?', in *Il giornale della donna*, yr. XV, no. 6, 15 March 1933.

Espressioni di stile sulla bandiera italiana, press release, Camera Nazionale della Moda Italiana, Milan 17 February 2004.

Caroline Evans, *Fashion at the Edge. Spectacle, Modernity and Deathliness*, Yale University Press, New Haven-London 2003.

Fashion for America, www.cfda.com/flash.html

'Fashion of the Times', in *The New York Times Magazine*, part II, fall 2000,
now in A̶B̶C̶D̶E̶ *Magazine: Viktor&Rolf par Viktor et Rolf*, première décennie, 2003.

'Flag issue: BCCI to approach Govt.', in *The Hindu*, 23 February 2005,
www.hindu.com/2005/02/23/stories/2005022302641900.htm

Bridget Foley, 'The Importance of Being Ralph', in *WWD*, section II, 14 May 2002.

Susannah Frankel, 'Fashion & Style', in *The Independent*, 17 June 2004.

Maria Luisa Frisa (ed.) with Francesco Bonami and Anna Mattirolo, *Italian Eyes.
Italian Fashion Photographs from 1951 to today*, Charta-Fondazione Pitti Immagine
Discovery, Milan-Florence 2005. Italian version *Lo sguardo italiano. Fotografie italiane
di moda dal 1951 a oggi*.

Paul Gilroy, *The Black Atlantic. Modernity and Double-Consciousness*, Verso,
London-New York 1993. Italian edition *The Black Atlantic. L'identità nera
tra modernità e doppia coscienza*, Meltemi, Rome 2003.

Masoud Golsorkhi, 'Editor's Letter. The Importance of Being Earnest', in *Tank*,
series IV, no. 1, February 2005.

Alison L. Goodrum, 'The First New Zealand Fashion Week Exhibition',
in *Fashion Theory*, yr. 8, no. 1, February 2004.

www.g-sus.com/

'Harry the Nazi. Prince's swastika outfit at party', in *The Sun*,
13 January 2005.

Dick Hebdige, *Subcultures. The Meaning of Style*, Methuen & Co., London 1979.
Italian edition *Sottocultura. Il fascino di uno stile innaturale*, Costa & Nolan,
Genoa 1983.

Dick Hebdige, *Hiding in the Light. On Images and Things*, Comedia-Routledge,
London 1988. Italian edition *La lambretta e il videoclip. Cose & consumi dell'immaginario
contemporaneo*, EDT, Turin 1991.

'Italian Ideas for Any South', in *American Vogue*, November 1951.

Naomi Klein, *No Logo: Taking Aim at the Brand Name Bullies*, Knopf, Toronto 2000.
Italian edition Trad it. *No logo. Economia globale e nuova contestazione*, Baldini&Castoldi,
Milan 2001.

www.l-a-m-b.com/

Ingrid Loschek, *Mother Earth Father Land. Not Uncontroversial - Eva Gronbach
and her Collections*, Goethe Institute, July 2004,
www.goethe.de/kug/kue/des/thm/en138594.htm

www.mambo.com.au/mambo.html

Richard Martin, 'Flag Clothing', in Tom Pendergast and Sara Pendergast (eds.),
St. James Encyclopedia of Popular Culture, vol. II, St. James Press, Detroit 2000.

Richard Martin, 'A Note: Art & Fashion, Viktor & Rolf', in *Fashion Theory*, yr. 3,
no. 1, March 1999.

Richard Martin and Viktor & Rolf, *Le regard noir*, no. 28,
www.smba.nl/shows/28/28.htm

Bruce Mau, *Life Style*, Phaidon, London 2002.

Angela McRobbie, *British Fashion Design. Rag Trade or Image Industry?*, Routledge, London-New York 1998. Italian version in Paola Colaiacomo, Vittoria C. Caratozzolo (eds.), *Mercanti di stile. Le culture della moda dagli anni '20 a oggi*, Editori Riuniti, Rome 2002.

William Middleton, 'New Amsterdam. Dutch design team Viktor & Rolf scores an international hit with its first collection of flag-waving ready-to-wear', in *Harper's Bazaar*, May 2000, p. 191-194, now in ~~ABCDE~~ *Magazine: Viktor&Rolf par Viktor et Rolf*, première décennie, 2003.

Nicholas Mirzoeff, *An Introduction to Visual Culture*, Routledge, London-New York 1999.

Maureen Molloy, 'Cutting-edge Nostalgia: New Zealand Fashion Design at the New Millennium', in *Fashion Theory*, yr. 8, no. 4, November 2004.

Franco Moschino and Lida Castelli (eds.), *X anni di kaos! 1983-1993*, Lybra, Milan 1993

Florence Müller, *JC de Castelbajac*, Assouline, Paris 2000.

www.novamatic.com/noki.htm

Oliviero Toscani al muro. L'arte visiva nella comunicazione pubblicitaria di United Colors of Benetton, Leonardo, Milan 1999.

Alistair O'Neill, *Cuttings and Pastings*, in Christopher Breward and Caroline Evans (eds.), *Fashion and Modernity*, Berg, Oxford-New York 2005.

Lorella Pagnucco Salvemini, *Benetton/Toscani. Storia di una avventura, 1984-2000*, Bolis, Azzano San Paolo 2002.

Michel Pastoureau, *Bleau. Histoire d'une couleur*, Seuil, Paris 2000. English edition

Blue. History of a Color, Princeton University Press, Princeton 2001.

Alberto Piccinini, 'Demolire la quarta parete del rock', in Giorgio Agamben (et al.), *I Situazionisti*, Manifestolibri, Rome 1991.

Ted Polhemus, *Street Style. From Sidewalk to Catwalk*, Thames and Hudson, London-New York 1994.

www.polo.com/history/history.asp?year=2002

www.reflag.co.uk/index.htm

Roger Sabin, '"I Won't Let That Dago By". Rethinking Punk and Racism', in Roger Sabin (ed.), *Punk Rock: So What? The Cultural Legacy of Punk*, Routledge, London 1999.

Cédric Saint-André Perrin and Paquita Paquin, 'La mode en capitales', in *Beaux Arts Magazine*, special issue *Qu'est-ce que la mode aujourd'hui?*, 2000.

Joanna Schlenzka, 'Another Corporate Assault', in *Another Magazine*, no. 8, spring-summer 2005.

Brian Sweeney, *Eight Reasons to Change the New Zealand Flag*, February 2004, www.nzflag.com/essay_sweeney.cfm

André Leon Talley, 'The Flag Bearers', in *American Vogue*, May 2000, now in *ABCDE Magazine: Viktor&Rolf par Viktor et Rolf*, première décennie, 2003.

www.thecorporation.com/index.php?page_id=2

www.tommy.com/about/rumor.aspx

Unbrandamerica.org, full-page advert in *The New York Times*, 3 July 2004.

'Unintentional Hurt. [Fashion] Magazine Chief Organiser Zou Xue issues statement of apology', in *Sina Entertainment*, 10 December 2001, www.zhaoweinetfamily.com/news_e/news_e455.html

Guido Vergani, *La Sala Bianca. Nascita della Moda Italiana*, Electa, Milan 1992.

Karen Walker, at www.nzflag.com/endorsements.cfm?i=46

Nicola White, *Reconstructing Italian Fashion. America and the Development of the Italian Fashion Industry*, Berg, Oxford-New York 2000.

Elizabeth Wilson, *Adorned in Dreams. Fashion and Modernity*, London, Virago, 1985.

Theodore Zeldin, 'A Manifesto for ...and?', in *...and?*, March 2002.

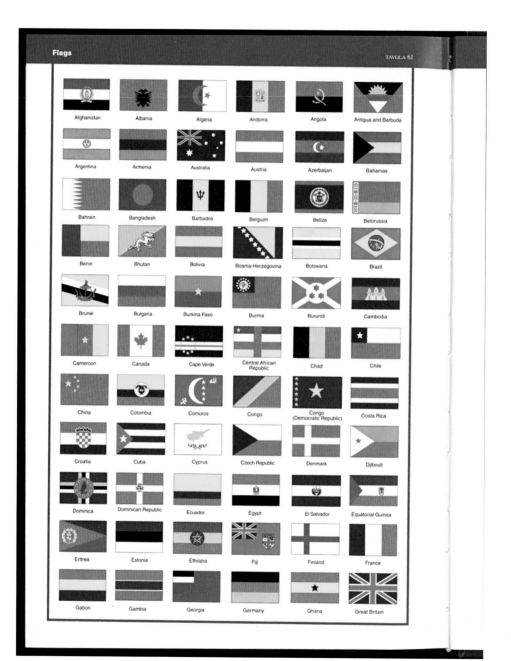

Afghanistan · Albania · Algeria · Andorra · Angola · Antigua and Barbuda

Argentina · Armenia · Australia · Austria · Azerbaijan · Bahamas

Bahrain · Bangladesh · Barbados · Belgium · Belize · Belorussia

Benin · Bhutan · Bolivia · Bosnia-Herzegovina · Botswana · Brazil

Brunei · Bulgaria · Burkina Faso · Burma · Burundi · Cambodia

Cameroon · Canada · Cape Verde · Central African Republic · Chad · Chile

China · Colombia · Comoros · Congo · Congo (Democratic Republic) · Costa Rica

Croatia · Cuba · Cyprus · Czech Republic · Denmark · Djibouti

Dominica · Dominican Republic · Ecuador · Egypt · El Salvador · Equatorial Guinea

Eritrea · Estonia · Ethiopia · Fiji · Finland · France

Gabon · Gambia · Georgia · Germany · Ghana · Great Britain

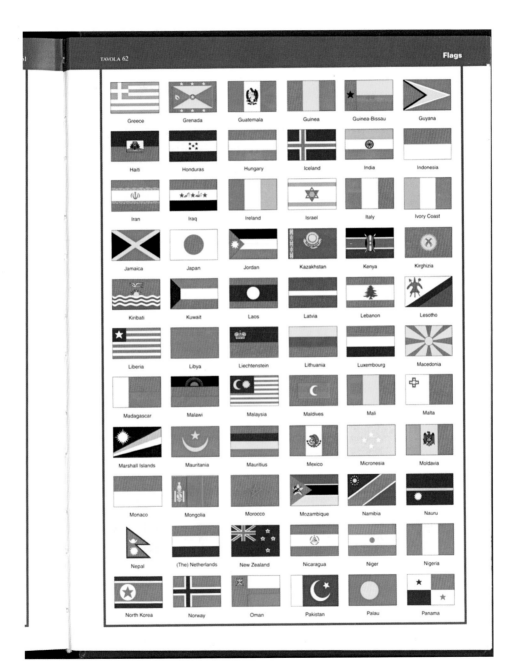

Greece Grenada Guatemala Guinea Guinea-Bissau Guyana

Haiti Honduras Hungary Iceland India Indonesia

Iran Iraq Ireland Israel Italy Ivory Coast

Jamaica Japan Jordan Kazakhstan Kenya Kirghizia

Kiribati Kuwait Laos Latvia Lebanon Lesotho

Liberia Libya Liechtenstein Lithuania Luxembourg Macedonia

Madagascar Malawi Malaysia Maldives Mali Malta

Marshall Islands Mauritania Mauritius Mexico Micronesia Moldavia

Monaco Mongolia Morocco Mozambique Namibia Nauru

Nepal (The) Netherlands New Zealand Nicaragua Niger Nigeria

North Korea Norway Oman Pakistan Palau Panama

Flags

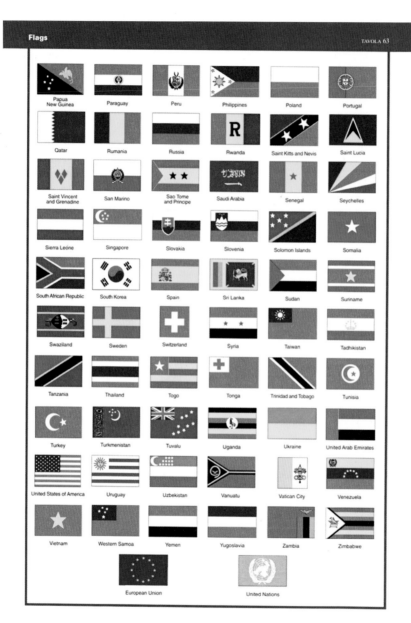

Papua New Guinea — Paraguay — Peru — Philippines — Poland — Portugal

Qatar — Rumania — Russia — Rwanda — Saint Kitts and Nevis — Saint Lucia

Saint Vincent and Grenadine — San Marino — Sao Tome and Principe — Saudi Arabia — Senegal — Seychelles

Sierra Leone — Singapore — Slovakia — Slovenia — Solomon Islands — Somalia

South African Republic — South Korea — Spain — Sri Lanka — Sudan — Suriname

Swaziland — Sweden — Switzerland — Syria — Taiwan — Tadhikistan

Tanzania — Thailand — Togo — Tonga — Trinidad and Tobago — Tunisia

Turkey — Turkmenistan — Tuvalu — Uganda — Ukraine — United Arab Emirates

United States of America — Uruguay — Uzbekistan — Vanuatu — Vatican City — Venezuela

Vietnam — Western Samoa — Yemen — Yugoslavia — Zambia — Zimbabwe

European Union — United Nations

Photolithograph
Fotolito Veneta, San Martino Buonalbergo (Verona)

Printed by
Grafiche Nardin, Ca' Savio - Cavallino - Treporti (Venice)
for Marsilio Editori® s.p.a., Venice

EDITION

YEAR

10 9 8 7 6 5 4 3 2 1

2005 2006 2007 2008 2009